DAVE WINFIELD
The 23 Million Dollar Man

DAVE WINFIELD
The 23 Million Dollar Man

GENE SCHOOR

5B

A SCARBOROUGH BOOK

STEIN AND DAY / *Publishers* / Scarborough House, Briarcliff Manor, N.Y. 10510

First published in 1982
Copyright © 1982 by Gene Schoor
All rights reserved
Designed by L.A. Ditizio
Printed in the United States of America
STEIN AND DAY/*Publishers*
Scarborough House
Briarcliff Manor, N.Y. 10510

Library of Congress Cataloging in Publication Data

Schoor, Gene.
    Dave Winfield, the 23 million dollar man.

    Includes index.
    1. Winfield, Dave, 1951–   .   2. Baseball
players—United States—Biography.   3. New York
Yankees (Baseball team)   I. Title.
GV865.W57S36   796.357'092'4 [B]   81-40807
ISBN 0-8128-2841-0   AACR2
ISBN 0-8128-6160-4 (pbk.)

To Fran Schoor,
my 23 million dollar wife

Contents

Illustrations

Dave in his new Yankee uniform

      ★   ★   ★   ★

Winfield with his high school team
The $23 Million Man as college pitcher
Winfield dunks a basketball
Winfield playing basketball for the University of
    Minnesota
Winfield stretches before stepping to the plate
The Winfield follow-through
Edging off second base
Running the bases
Stealing second
Close play at third
Crossing the plate
Dave starts batting swing
With Mike Schmidt at 1980 All-Star Game
Riding New York subway
With Yankee owner George Steinbrenner
Trying on new Yankee cap, with Reggie Jackson
In the Yankee locker room
Tagged out at third
Where the action is

(frontispiece and pages 73 to 80)

Acknowledgments

I wish to thank all those individuals and organizations whose marvelous contributions helped in preparing this volume.

A special note of thanks to my good friend Don Riley, the outstanding sports columnist of the *St. Paul Pioneer Press* for his aid. . . .

To Bill Peterson, Director of the Jimmy Lee Playground, St. Paul, Minnesota

Joe Janitschke, Police Department, White Bear, Minnesota

Jim Fritsche, Baseball, Basketball Coach, Central High School, St. Paul, Minnesota

Dr. Edwin Haislet, Former Executive Director, University of Minnesota Alumni Association

Jim Williams, Assistant Basketball Coach, University of Minnesota

Bob Petersen, Sports Information Director, University of Minnesota

Tom Greenhoe, Wendell Vandersluis . . . Sports Information Department, University of Minnesota

And to my colleague Howard Liss. *Minneapolis Star* . . . Sports Editor

A special note of thanks to Mrs. Arline Winfield . . .

I also wish to thank the following for photos supplied from their files:

Bob Chandler, San Diego Padres, Public Relations Director

University of Minnesota Athletic Department

Los Angeles Times, Sports Department

St. Paul Pioneer Press, Sports Department

New York Daily News

Wide World Photos

Jim Fritsche, Central High School, St. Paul, Minnesota

1

The Rookie
Had Tools

He was a grass-green, twenty-one-year-old kid just off the University of Minnesota campus when he reported to the San Diego Padres on June 19, 1973. Seemingly, he was in the right town, but with the wrong team at the wrong time. Dave Winfield, at 6 feet 6 inches and 225 pounds, would have looked more natural as a tight end with the San Diego Chargers of the National Football League, and might well have been a rookie trying to get in shape for the football season. However, Padres manager Don Zimmer knew he was getting a baseball player, especially after watching his newest acquisition take his cuts in batting practice. Zim nodded approvingly at the line drives the young man powered in practice and decided to play Winfield that very night.

Only a few days earlier, Winfield and his Golden Gophers had been eliminated from the National Collegiate Athletic Association (NCAA) World Series by the University of Southern California. Minnesota, aided and abetted by Winfield's 9-1 record as a pitcher and his .385 batting average, had won the Big Ten title and swept into the semifinals before being edged out by the Trojans. Nobody objected strenuously when he was named Most Valuable Player (MVP) of the NCAA tournament, nor to his selection as a college All-American.

On the strength of his showing as a senior, and his overall record as a college player, Winfield had been selected by the Padres in the draft; he was the fourth player chosen in the first round. He had also been scouted extensively by representatives of every major league team. The verdict was practically unanimous. Dave Winfield was a marvelous athlete and a great major league prospect.

"He has more physical tools than any free agent we have ever signed," said Peter Bavasi, general manager of the Padres. "He can do the five things you look for in a player with super potential: run, throw, field, hit for average, and hit with power."

Admittedly, Winfield was nervous in his debut. He had to prove he was worth the money San Diego had paid him. His agent, Marvin Milkes, had negotiated a contract that called for something over $75,000, the bulk of it as a bonus. At the time, before major league free agency had sent paychecks soaring to unbelievable numbers, that was considered a handsome bonus for playing a kid's game. And then there was the matter of his personal pride. As a college player, he had been Mr. Big, but press clippings couldn't buy instant success. He had to prove that he had major league ability. Was he ready to make the jump from college to the majors? If so, at which position, outfield or pitcher?

"I signed a major league contract," Winfield said philosophically before departing for the West Coast. "They don't have to keep me in San Diego if they believe I'm not ready to play there. I could wind up in Hawaii of the Pacific Coast League before the season is over." Then he added, "If I don't make it as an outfielder, I assume they'll try me as a pitcher."

To a certain extent that decision had already been made by the Padres front office. "We want him as an everyday player," said player personnel director Bob Fontaine. "With his ability to run and hit and throw, he can be more valuable to us if he can break into the lineup and stay there."

Winfield joined a team already overstocked with outfielders of varying talent, among them Jerry Morales, Clarence Gaston, Gene Locklear, Johnny Grubb, Leron Lee, and Dave Marshall, the latter strictly a pinch hitter. Marshall was sent to the minors to make room for Winfield.

However, it didn't seem to matter much who came or went. The Padres were wallowing in last place in the National League West, 20 games behind front-running Los Angeles, with the season somewhat more than two months gone. They had dropped nine straight prior to Winfield's arrival on the scene.

It would be straight out of Frank Merriwell to report that Winfield stepped in and reversed the Padres fortunes. It would also be untrue. A meager crowd of 5,338 watched the home team drop its tenth straight to the Houston Astros, 7-3, but they also saw a few things that stirred some vestiges of hope for the future. It wasn't merely Winfield's first major league base hit, a single on which he eventually scored. His fielding also brought forth a few smiles.

In the first inning, Cesar Cedeno banged one to left, where Winfield had been installed. The rookie played the ball by the book, getting his body in front of the drive and then throwing accurately to his cutoff man, holding Cedeno to a single. Such good fielding in itself was a San Diego rarity. In the eighth he sprinted into the corner to run down Doug Rader's potential extra-base blow and fired a strike to second, gunning down the runner's bid for a stretched double.

"An outstanding play, an outstanding throw," Zimmer said enthusiastically. It had been a long time since Zim had anything in a Padres uniform to get enthusiastic about.

Winfield got another hit in his next game, and following that he got three, including his first big league home run. Winfield scored the club's only runs in a 12-2 loss to Houston. By then the Padres coaches had sized up the newcomer with the size-13 shoes, and while they liked what they saw overall, they felt there was room for improvement.

Batting coach Bob Skinner had observed a hitch in Winfield's swing. The rookie dropped his hands slightly before he brought the bat around. Winfield was also slow getting out of the batter's box after making contact. However, for the time being, Skinner was reluctant to begin working on Winfield's plate performance.

Skinner pointed out that players troubled by a hitch usually have difficulty with fastballs, but Winfield had very quick hands. The home run he hit was pitched in tight, a normal brushback by the pitcher, but Winfield had gotten around on the ball successfully. Also, he was surprisingly fast once he gained full stride. He could really steam down the line. As proof, Skinner cited the stats so far: three of Winfield's first five hits had been infield singles. Therefore, nobody was going to mess around with Winfield as long as he continued to produce, both at bat and in the outfield.

That was a mistake. In fact, the Padres made several mistakes with Winfield during his rookie season. Evidently the Padres had no intention of using Winfield as an "everyday player," in spite of the initial press blurbs. Obviously, Zimmer had been instructed to pick the spots for Winfield, to platoon him against lefthanded pitchers. So, although Winfield continued to hover around the .300 mark, he was still relatively untested. It seemed that somebody in the executive suite didn't think Winfield could hit major league pitching consistently. Such strategy made absolutely no sense. As one San Diego staff writer put it, "This is a hell of a way to run a franchise."

"I know people think I'm an idiot," Zimmer said in an interview. "Here I have a team 30 games out of first place, I have a great-looking new kid hitting .300 and I don't use him. I would like to play him every day for a month and see if he belongs here or not. Maybe he does, but right now we honestly don't know."

Zimmer acknowledged the hitch in Winfield's swing and the problems it posed, but confessed he was afraid to turn Skinner loose on his rookie. "Bob was going to work with him," Zimmer said, "but I stopped him. I said he couldn't do it while he's hitting so high. If he goes into a slump, we'll be blamed for it. They'll all say we confused him."

Winfield was already confused enough, but he shrugged his sloping shoulders and obeyed orders. "I hit righthanded pitchers in college, and I wouldn't be afraid to face a Tom Seaver or a Bob Gibson, but I'll do whatever they want me to do," he told reporters.

As if to prove his statement, Winfield started an August 14th game against the New York Mets because southpaw Jerry Koosman was on the mound. In the fourth inning Winfield's single drove in a run. In the fifth inning, facing righthander John Strohmayer with two mates aboard, Winfield clouted one into the left field seats for a three-run homer. As it turned out, that was Winfield's third and last home run of the season.

Ten days later, Winfield showed a new facet of his versatility. He

6

played first base in place of Nate Colbert, who had suffered a painful spike wound. He not only played the position well, but his two-run triple was a major contribution to the Padres' 5-3 victory over Montreal.

But for Don Zimmer the season was a nightmare, and he deserved a better fate. He was always one of the best, on and off the field, a scrapper who never quit. He had been in the Brooklyn farm system as a shortstop, waiting in the wings until Peewee Reese conceded to age. In 1956 Zim was beaned by an errant pitch and almost died. Thirteen days later, after two operations, he was still unconscious, and it took almost six months before he could speak normally.

The tough, tubby little man with the big wad of Red Ball chewing tobacco lumped in his cheek returned to the baseball wars, only to suffer another beaning a couple of years later. The ball crunched against his cheekbone and Zim suffered a detached retina. He was laid low for another five months, yet he kept coming back, knowing that another blow on the head might be fatal.

Don Zimmer had paid his dues, both as a player and manager, in the major and minor leagues. In 1972 he had been called up from Salt Lake City, where he was managing, to take over for the Padres after skipper Preston Gomez was fired. That year the club finished sixth. In 1973 he was at the helm all season. The club won 60 and lost 102, 39 games out, and ended in sixth place again.

Sixth place is the charitable way to indicate the team's final standing. There are only six teams in the National League West. Everyone knows what happens to managers who finish last. They are told to seek employment somewhere else.

Montreal manager Gene Mauch, who had used Zimmer as his third base coach in 1971, said of his former aide, "There isn't a manager in the majors, Walter Alston [of the Los Angeles Dodgers] included, who could win any more games with that San Diego club than Zimmer has won."

As for Dave Winfield, his rookie year was a season of neither triumph nor disaster. He showed flashes of power and he certainly could field his position, but in the main, all of 1973 was a learning experience. And even though he hit safely in his first half-dozen major league games, Dave knew in his heart he had a long, long way to go before he qualified as an authentic major leaguer.

"It's incredible, this being part of a major league team," said Dave. "It takes time to get adjusted to the game and to the life style, but I'm accepted and that helps."

At least that's what he told his mother and grandmother on the telephone—and there were many calls home. It does take time to adjust to a new situation, but the bit about being accepted was a good deal exaggerated. As he would say later, it was the contrary that was true, and it was giving him a most difficult time.

"I learned right away," he said later, "that big league baseball can be a cold business. It's not like college ball. My first three months with the Padres were just about the hardest months in my life. The older players were not about to help me out. Everybody was fighting for a job on the team . . . and I was there taking a job away from some veteran. Everybody was very cool and distant."

"I didn't know anything about the National League," he said, years later. "I was seeing pitches I'd never seen before, I was playing in a ball park the size of an airport, I'd get my legs all tangled up in the outfield, I was holding my hands too low on the bat, I was hitching my swing, overstriding, overswinging. I'd been primarily a pitcher, now I was an outfielder. I was thrown into a sink-or-swim situation. I learned to swim the hard way."

His rookie statistics were completely ordinary. In 56 games he batted .277, with four doubles, one triple, three home runs, and 12 runs batted in. He struck out 19 times in 141 at-bats, or approximately once every seven and a half appearances. He walked a dozen times and scored nine runs.

It was only a fair beginning, yet one that showed some promise. But not enough promise to indicate that he would someday become a player worth more than twenty million dollars to another team in another league.

2

Growing Up,
and Up, and Up ...

On October 3, 1951, David Mark Winfield was born, the second son of Frank and Arline Winfield. David's big brother, Steve, was then some fourteen months old.

Home was then, and still is for Arline, a modest house on Carroll Avenue in the Midway section of St. Paul, Minnesota. Dave was three years old when his parents divorced and his father moved away. Arline took a job in the audio-visual department of the St. Paul public school system, a position she still holds. The responsibility of raising her boys rested squarely on her shoulders, but she has always admitted that she had plenty of help from her own mother, affectionately known as "Grandma Jessie."

"They were good boys," Arline often recalls. "Sometimes they got out of line like normal kids will, but I had a sure cure."

Arline's "cure" was a lilac bush growing in the yard. She would send them out to cut a switch from the bush, and then she would rap them smartly across the legs with it. But that wasn't often necessary. Using quiet reasoning, she made them understand the difficulties of keeping a household together without the presence of a father figure.

Dave says that he learned a lot from those switchings, but that he learned a lot more from the way his mother talked with her two boys. She would reason with them and explain things to them, such as the absence of a father in the house, or the budget that didn't permit buying things that other kids had.

"When the boys were growing up," says Arline Winfield, "I didn't have enough money to get some of the things they wanted, but we weren't that dependent on money. Some kids have a lot of things you can buy with money, but they don't have love and consideration. In a lot of ways they were poorer than we were."

A thinking woman, a sensible and sensitive woman, Arline Winfield gave her children the thing she had most of: love. And she was repaid in the same coin.

"What I am now," Dave Winfield says, "I owe to my mother. My motivation came from home."

Certainly Dave's love for kids, his devotion to their welfare, is an echo of his mother's love for her children. It also shows itself in the love the two brothers, Dave and Steve, have for each other, and in the love they have and show for their mother. Home, for Dave Winfield, wherever baseball may take him, is still on Carroll Avenue in St. Paul.

There's a grandmother in the picture, too, Grandma Jessie.

Grandma Jessie was born in Tennessee, but lived there for only six weeks. Then her family wandered all over the country. Her father just couldn't stay in one place for very long. Jessie finally married and gave birth to her eight children in St. Paul. She lived just across the street from her daughter, Arline, and that was a blessing—particularly when Steve and Dave were just toddlers.

"I don't know where I'd be without Mom," says Arline. "I took the kids to her house so that I could go to work. And she took good care of them. It was the only way I could continue working."

Grandma Jessie taught the boys a few things, too, things that stuck with them for a long time.

Dave Winfield, struggling in his first few weeks with the Padres, often phoned Grandma Jessie for advice and now recalls one of her favorite phrases: "Boy, you've got to work, have patience, sacrifice, and use your head."

"Well," he adds, "I worked like she said and I always tried to keep my head."

"That woman," Arline says of her mother, "deserves a crown in heaven, a star in heaven. I just wouldn't know what I would have done without her. It would have been impossible."

Money was always a problem. Arline couldn't afford a car, and even years later, when Dave was in college and an All-American baseball star, he too used a bus to get where he wanted to go.

"When the boys were growing up," says Arline, "I always was proud of their ball-playing and tried to be at every ball game they played. If I had a dollar for every game I saw, I guess I'd be very rich today," she laughs.

"Most important to the way the boys grew up was the fact that I didn't have to worry about where they were and what they were doing while I was at work. Both Steve and Dave loved sports so much, I always knew they were at the playground until I got home. I was and shall be always grateful to Mr. Peterson at the playground for his kindness with both boys. Bill Peterson taught them discipline. He had some tough rules and they had to abide by them."

As the Winfield boys grew older they were drawn toward the Oxford Playground, located just down the block from home. It was run by Bill Peterson, the director, and his assistant Joe Janitschke. Bill, a 5-foot-11-inch 230-pound bear of a man, had played varsity football, hockey, and baseball at St. Paul's Central High School, then later was a fine catcher for the University of Minnesota baseball team. The last time anybody looked he was still there, supervisor of Municipal Athletics at Oxford Playground, only now it's called the Jimmy Lee Playground. And he is still showing youngsters how to achieve a level swing of the bat and how to get in front of a ground ball.

Joe Janitschke had played baseball, football, and basketball at Minnehaha Academy in St. Paul, and he too worked with the kids. Joe is no longer with the playground; for some years he has been a police officer in White Bear, Minnesota, a suburb of the Twin Cities of Minneapolis and St. Paul. He has a story about Dave that he loves to tell.

During the American Legion championship tournament, Dave and his teammates were in a Coon Rapids hotel. They were scheduled to play against the Coon Rapids team the following morning, and the boys were gathered in the hotel lobby. Dave sauntered over to one of the Coon Rapids players.

"Hey, you ever hear of Dave Winfield?" he asked. The kid shook his head. So did a few others standing nearby. "Well, by tomorrow, you'll hear a lot about him," Dave said, and walked away.

"He always was a cocky kid," Joe chuckles.

Yet, at that time Steve was the better athlete, since he was taller, stronger, and heavier. But it was Dave who had more confidence and wasn't shy about showing it. Even then he made sure everyone within earshot knew that some day he was going to play major league baseball.

Very early in life both boys came to understand what it meant to be black. In those years the black population of Minneapolis–St. Paul was estimated at somewhere between 9 and 11 percent of the total population, and was grouped into a few areas. Midway was one such area. However, although Dave's immediate neighborhood was black, the majority of the students at his elementary school, the I. J. Hill School, were white.

In class, Dave would listen to the teacher talk about history, but she never uttered a word about black history, for the simple reason that no such subject was taught in the public schools at that time.

"When the teacher mentioned Africa, I'd kind of slide down in my seat," Dave recalled. "The white kids would laugh or giggle, and I would get a feeling of shame."

The stigma burned deeply into both boys, especially Steve. Steve probably had more raw talent than Dave and might have gone on to a brighter athletic career than his kid brother, except that he became completely involved as a black militant in the civil rights movement. One way or another, his dedication to the cause impeded his progress as an athlete. But he has no regrets, and today he revels in the reflected glory of Dave's accomplishments.

Dave, in his own way, was no less militant, but he managed to keep his feelings under control thanks to his admiration and deep feelings for Bill Peterson. Bill had become a surrogate father, a confidant, a man Dave could take his problems to and find a willing ear. Both Peterson and Janitschke are white.

Dave and Steve always attended the same schools. After the I. J. Hill School, they went to Marshall Junior High, and then Central High. Dave's athletic ability wasn't much in evidence until after his sophomore year in high school, when he began to grow as if his pituitary gland was on a rampage. Almost overnight, it seemed, he shot up more than four inches and added some heft to his frame. Only then was he noticed by Jim Fritsche, Central High's baseball and basketball coach.

In his school days Fritsche was quite an athlete. He played basketball and baseball at Humboldt High School in St. Paul and was outstanding even then. Fritsche was a big kid, well over six feet tall, weighing something over two hundred pounds, and it was evident that he would make a career of sports.

"I wanted to become a professional baseball player," Fritsche said of his early daydreams, "but I couldn't hit a curve ball."

It was his own honest self-evaluation that made him decide that whatever future he had was in basketball. He was one of the key players who took Humboldt High to the Minnesota State high school championship in 1949. From there it was on to Hamline University in St. Paul, a school with a national reputation for its basketball teams. Four years later he was drafted by the National Basketball Association and he played under coach Claire Bee, who was one of college basketball's legends when he coached championship teams at Long Island University.

In 1954–55, basketball players did not earn salaries that had six figures with no decimal points between the zeroes. Fritsche's paycheck was about six thousand dollars per season, but he was on the same court with some of the superstars of the past, giants of the early NBA years, such as Bob Cousy of the Boston Celtics, George Mikan of the then Minneapolis Lakers, Dolph Shayes of the Syracuse Nationals, Carl Braun of the New York Knicks, Bill Sharman of the Celtics, and a few others whose names are in basketball's Hall of Fame. When a job opened up at Central High, he took it. The money was adequate and at least he was home.

Fritsche had little varsity basketball material to work with at Central. He had overlooked David Winfield for a few valid reasons: first, until his junior year, Dave was just a kid who sometimes shot a few baskets for fun at the Oxford playground. The game didn't interest him much.

13

Second, he had only just begun to grow out of his clothing and he wasn't yet an imposing figure; he was just average. Dave didn't even go out for the baseball team until his junior year.

"He had the raw talent," Fritsche has said in retrospect. "But he was very late developing. Most superstars become heroes early on. Not Dave. I'm amazed at his development."

Dave didn't go out for the Central High baseball team until his junior year, and not until he was a senior did he show up for basketball. He had already proved his potential as a pitcher with an American Legion team, coached, incidentally, by Bill Peterson. Dave's control was fair and he had practically nothing in the way of a curve, but his fastball was live and moving.

Steve was a senior playing first base when Dave made the team as a junior. Dave was skittish. A fluke hit or an error would upset him, and then Fritsche would stroll slowly out toward the mound to calm him. When he got there he always found two Winfields: Dave and Steve—who had ambled over from his position. Steve never said a word. He just looked at Fritsche, at Dave, and smiled a lot.

At the end of the season curiosity was eating at Fritsche. He had to know exactly why Steve wanted to be present, uninvited, at comparatively meaningless conferences.

"I just wanted to hear what you had to say," Steve explained.

Fritsche finally figured it out. "Steve knew Dave would settle down," Fritsche said. "He'd played ball with Dave all his life. He knew his brother far better than I did. His presence helped. I think it was a testimonial to their closeness as brothers. It was a beautiful thing to see."

In his senior year Dave was the star pitcher of an otherwise inept Central High baseball team. Bill Peterson, merely as an observer, assessed Fritsche's aggregation as "one of the poorest teams I've ever seen." That they made it into the state regionals was due to Dave's work. Central posted a 5-3 record, and it was Dave's pitching and hitting that took the team that far.

On June 4, 1969, Dave Winfield's name was in the St. Paul and Minneapolis newspapers. Coon Rapids, a "bedroom community" of the Twin Cities, also had reason to mention him, much to their sorrow. The previous day Dave had risen to the heights. All he did was fire a

13-strikeout, extra-inning, no-hit, no-run game, which Central pulled out, 1-0, on an infield error. Yet, in a way, no one was really surprised. The year before, Dave had been voted Most Valuable Player in the State American Legion tournament. This year he was even better.

The finals pitted Central against a pretty good South St. Paul High School team, and the only pitcher other than Dave who might have stood up to them was Joe Tschida. But Central's catcher was injured and Tschida was versatile enough to take his place behind the plate. That meant Dave would have to pitch again the very next day with no rest at all. Dave gave it his best try but his arm was tired. South St. Paul beat him, 5-3.

Dave also played basketball in his senior year, and once again the pattern repeated itself. He started slowly, then found his own strengths and capitalized on them. In this case Dave's shot left something to be desired, and he was no ball of fire on defense, but how that guy could rebound! He would kangaroo up and over everyone to grab the ball off the boards, averaging a dozen or more per game.

Coach Fritsche described Dave's leaping ability in glowing terms. "It bordered on the unbelievable," he said. "Dave was easy to coach, he listened, he paid attention, he learned. I enjoyed his company. I remember Dave Winfield as a young man with pride, never pushy, a fun kid, never fresh or sassy. He always gave me one hundred percent."

Dave made All-State as a high school basketball player, too.

The baseball scouts were already knocking at his door. The Boston Red Sox, for one, drafted him right out of high school. However, the University of Minnesota offered him an athletic scholarship. For the first time in all his tender years Dave Winfield was faced with a tough decision.

Sure, he wanted to be a professional baseball player. It had always been his dream. But there were some drawbacks. Undoubtedly the Red Sox would send him to the minors for seasoning, probably in a Class-A or Double-A league. But he'd heard how blacks were treated in some small towns and he had no intention of becoming a second-class citizen. That wasn't good enough for a proud young black like David Mark Winfield.

The University of Minnesota seemed to promise a good deal more. Dave was mature enough to realize the value of a college education, especially for a black man, and now he had the opportunity to carve out some sort of career for the inevitable time when his playing days would be over.

And there was also the obvious opportunity to gain playing experience in college, which, he figured, should be at least the equivalent of the low minors. Some colleges, such as Arizona State and the University of Southern California, were practically of high minor league caliber in their own right. At Minnesota he'd be tutored by Dick Siebert, one of the finest college coaches in the country, a man who had won his share of Big Ten baseball championships.

Besides, Steve was already attending the university, and he was doing quite well there. It might be a kick to be with his brother in college.

Sure enough he opted for college, but only after long discussions with Steve, with Arline, with Grandma Jessie, with Bill Peterson, and finally with Jim Fritsche. They all told him more or less what he already knew, that if he was any good he'd find out for certain playing college ball, and the education he'd get along the way would develop him as a man.

It was a choice Dave Winfield never had cause to regret.

3

"Biggest Mistake
of My Life"

The term "living legend" is much abused, but no other phrase is applicable when discussing the reverence accorded Dick Siebert during his coaching career at the University of Minnesota. He was a demigod, the epitome of the All-American success story, "Mr. Baseball" as far as his peers in the Big Ten were concerned. His players and associates simply called him "Chief." The average Twin Cities citizen looked upon him as the home town boy who made good. Dave Winfield saw Siebert's help as invaluable on his road to the major leagues. If he couldn't maximize his talents under Siebert's coaching, then no one else could teach him any more either, and why bother?

Siebert began his career in organized baseball as an outstanding pitcher at St. Paul's Concordia High School, then continued at Concordia Junior College, moving from there to Concordia Seminary in St. Louis to prepare for the ministry. A profoundly religious man, Siebert felt initially that his calling was the priesthood, but at the seminary he began to experience grave doubts. He felt himself torn by his love for the church and an equally deep love for baseball. An intelligent, reasoning man, Siebert understood that anything less than total dedication to the church was unthinkable in a priest and he put aside life as a clergyman in favor of flannel uniforms.

In 1932 Siebert began his professional career, which included minor league journeys through Ohio, Pennsylvania, and New York. He played in various farm chains, including those belonging to the Brooklyn Dodgers, Chicago Cubs, and St. Louis Cardinals. Finally, in 1938, he was signed by the Philadelphia Athletics. By then his arm had long been lame and he was a first baseman, a pretty good, consistent batter, one of the quality players in the American League.

"It was one of the big thrills of my life to play under Connie Mack," Siebert said. And there were other big moments in his career: playing in the 1943 All-Star game, being selected for the 1945 All-Star squad, only to see that game canceled due to wartime restrictions, spoiling Bob Feller's bid for a no-hitter early in the fireballer's career, finishing his career in 1946 with an eminently respectable .290 lifetime average.

Siebert became a radio sportscaster with station WTCN in Minneapolis, and then, in 1947, was hired as head baseball coach by the University of Minnesota. Long before Dave Winfield arrived on the scene, Dick Siebert had carved his niche in college baseball.

Over the years honors cascaded upon him: president of the American College Baseball Coaches Association, Coach of the Year in 1956 and 1960, winner of the NCAA championship in 1956, 1960, and 1964, winner of the Big Ten crown in 1956, 1958, 1959, 1960, 1964, 1968, and 1969. He would win two more titles while Winfield was a student, in 1970 and 1973.

As a freshman, Winfield was used exclusively as a pitcher, and although freshmen were eligible to play with the varsity, he didn't. But he made his presence felt by going 4-0 with one perfect game. It was not a performance to be dismissed, but Winfield did express some disappointment.

"I didn't play when I wasn't pitching," he noted. "Still, I hit about .300 just as a pitcher." Winfield thought he might have been used, even sparingly, in the outfield, at shortstop or at first base. He certainly had the versatility.

Organized baseball was the great love of Dave Winfield's life. He hadn't had his fill as a freshman, and there was another outlet in the form of the Metro Collegiate Summer League. Winfield enlisted eagerly, and he was used not only as a pitcher but as a right fielder when he wasn't on the mound. He batted .373, but that wasn't the big story. Teammates and adversaries alike looked at his six-foot-six, towering figure with awe. He was a titan on the pitching mound, blowing away the opposition with his deliveries. After eight weeks of competition, Dave Winfield's presence overshadowed all others. Metro Leaguers offered a variety of opinions on Winfield, all of them very flattering.

"Any game Winfield pitches is a foregone conclusion," said John Peterson, a .405 hitter. "He throws harder than anyone we had on the varsity last season."

From third baseman Bob Warhol came this evaluation: "Even if the hitter knows his fastball is coming, it's still good enough. He has much better than average speed for a Big Ten pitcher."

Catcher Tim Grice evaluated the development in Winfield: "During the spring his curve wasn't his best pitch. Now it's improved. He also added a slider. Those pitches make his fastball even more over-powering."

"He's one of the best prospects to come to the university in a long time," said assistant coach Jerry Kindall. "He has a real quality of fierce, competitive spirit and he wants badly to be the best. A lot of players with that much ability will tend to let down in practice, but that's not true of Dave."

Perhaps the highest accolade came from teammate Jeff Ward, also a pitcher. "We're going to win tonight," he said one day. "Winfield's pitching."

Winfield's Metro stats told it all: he won 8 games and lost none, with an .091 earned run average. Hitters faced him reluctantly. One was quoted, "Out there on the mound, Winfield looks as if he'll either strike you out or kill you."

That particular statement reflected Winfield's approach to pitching. "A pitcher has to have that attitude," he said. "You've got to go out there knowing you'll get the batter out no matter what he thinks. You've got to think that you're better than the hitter. If you have it on your mind that you're going to throw it by him, that's exactly what you'll do."

As a batter, Winfield reversed that strategy. "I don't take too many pitches," he said. "If the ball is anywhere near the strike zone, I'll hit it."

Using that formula, in one game during the summer Winfield went 3-for-4, with two of his blows being home runs over the left field fence.

Contrary to his own beliefs, Winfield actually had made an impression during his freshman basketball stint. George Hanson, then the varsity coach, thought he had possibilities, especially in view of the fact that Winfield had played only one year of high school ball. Winfield, however, wasn't interested at that time. There was always the anticipation of an injury which might interfere with baseball, and if he was going to get a jersey and shorts, it would be only for intramural basketball, and then just to keep in shape for baseball. He was in no mood to jeopardize his future, especially after his spectacular advancement as a pitcher, and his satisfactory 3.3 grade average in his studies.

Temporarily at least, Winfield's decision seemed to be the right one. As early as January 1971, after the Gophers had taken the Big Ten title the previous spring, coach Siebert was asked, "Do you see an outstanding young man coming up this year?"

Siebert pondered the question and replied, "Well, not unless you're talking about Dave Winfield, that righthanded, six-foot-six sophomore pitcher from St. Paul. He's a fine prospect as a pitcher and he hits the ball with power. I think he could go all the way to the big leagues."

On the surface Siebert's statement seemed mild considering Winfield's showing in the Metro League. The strapping young pitcher had gone 4-0 as a freshman and then 8-0 in summer ball. He hadn't been defeated yet. Why then did Siebert downplay a potential star? What did Winfield have to do to prove himself?

Perhaps Siebert's reluctance was due to the stupid thing Winfield did. It was a lapse of common sense that might well have destroyed him totally as a student and future college athlete. He had everything going for him and, by his own admission, he almost blew it.

On August 29, 1970, the following item appeared in the newspaper:

Two St. Paul youths, both University of Minnesota students, were charged in Hennepin County Municipal Court today with the theft of a snowblower from a Minneapolis store.

20

They are David Winfield, 18, of Carroll Avenue, and Jeffrey Douglas, 21, of Fuller Avenue. They were arrested behind Wilson's Hardware Store on Washington Avenue SE.

They were released on bonds of $1,500 each. A preliminary hearing was scheduled for September 22.

Winfield, a sophomore, has an 8-0 record as a baseball pitcher and last year played on the freshman baseball team.

Police said they saw Winfield carrying a box containing the snowblower to a car where Douglas was waiting.

Why did he do it? Stealing wasn't Dave Winfield's style. It could be noted cynically that he wasn't a good thief since he was grabbed by the police right outside the hardware store, caught red-handed, still carrying the unopened carton. What was he thinking of to pull such an addle-brained stunt?

Was the rent due and did he need quick cash? Was it a case of falling into bad company? Was he backsliding into the ways of some black young people, whose main purpose in life seemed to be "Get Whitey," and who ripped off whatever seemed easiest and handiest? Well, Dave Winfield was something of a black militant, sporting an Afro and chin beard, but he soft-pedalled it. There seemed to be a world of difference between Dave and Steve—Steve Winfield was so grief-stricken by the assassination of Martin Luther King, Jr. that he quit the university to devote his energies to underprivileged youngsters, particularly blacks.

Even today Winfield refuses to offer an alibi. He prefers instead to keep his reasons to himself, whatever they are. He spent three days in jail, days of agonized soul-searching, before the bond money arrived. The entire incident was traumatic and will probably haunt him for the rest of his life.

"I was sure that was the end of my scholarship at the university," he said later. "I felt that everything I had thought of and dreamed of was gone. Goodbye scholarship. Goodbye baseball career. Goodbye everything."

Even more unbearable was the impact he knew the incident would have on his mother. "I felt bad about what my mother had to go through.

21

I still feel bad, rotten, when I think of it. She gave me everything, love, affection, encouragement, everything. She was so proud of me, so proud whenever I did well in baseball, basketball, anything. Now I have to prove I'm not a bad dude."

Regardless of subsequent exemplary behavior, Winfield brooded over the consequences of his act; he began to understand how he had stained his reputation. He said, "Every time you go to fill out an application for a job or something, you have to put down that you've been in jail."

But Winfield wasn't totally alone. He had friends who knew that one aberration need not be indicative of a person's total character. They came to court to pay tribute to him as a basically good man who had never been in trouble with the law before and probably never would again. The judge seemed impressed and since it was a first offense, sentence was suspended.

Evaluating the three-day jail ordeal, Winfield made no bones about his ultimate salvation. "Man, I know if it wasn't for sports, I'd be back on the streets. It would have been so easy."

Perhaps, then, that was why coach Dick Siebert seemed somewhat hesitant about singing the praises of such a promising candidate for his Gophers. The young man had, figuratively, been caught with his hand in the till. True, it was his first brush with the law, and anyone was entitled to one mistake. Siebert was as willing as the next man to give him a fair shake, not to hold anything against him. It was up to Winfield.

For the next few months Dave kept a low profile. True to his word, he did not try for the varsity when the basketball season arrived. Instead he played with an intramural team colorfully dubbed the Soulful Strutters. It was a surprisingly good team and they won the university championship. Winfield wasn't the captain but he was certainly the spark plug.

Then the baseball season arrived, and with the warm weather Winfield seemed to blossom. There was no question in anyone's mind that he would make the team, merely what his final stats would be. It didn't take very long for Winfield to show his coach that he was a pitcher to be reckoned with.

Minnesota opened the Big Ten season with a double-header against Michigan State and Dave started the opener. He lost it, 2-0, on a pair of unearned runs. It would be redundant to say that a team can't win when it doesn't score, and Michigan State's stylish lefty, Rob Chandler, threw a three-hit shutout at the Gophers. State's runs came on a pair of walks, a wild pitch, and two errors.

In the second game the Gophers were leading, 4-3, when State threatened in the sixth inning. With two out and runners on first and second, Siebert went to his bullpen, where none other than Dave Winfield was warming up. He worked the count to 3-and-2 on the Spartans' Rob Ellis, then struck him out. Then he retired the State batters in the next inning, and since it was a seven-inning game, Dave got credit for the save.

All things considered, Winfield's baseball season as a sophomore was a good one. He won 8 and lost 3, with an earned run average of 1.48, which was quite all right with coach Siebert, although he professed that he still didn't know how good Dave was. Certainly Dave had come a long way. Counting freshman and sophomore stints, plus the Metro League, he had won 20 and lost only 3, a record any young pitcher would gladly embrace.

Winfield fully intended to return to basketball with the Soulful Strutters at the start of his junior year, and he did—for a while. What happened afterward can only be termed one of the darkest days in the history of college basketball. It was an ugly incident involving players from the University of Minnesota and Ohio State University. Dave Winfield was in on it. The event has been covered extensively, in sequence photographs supplied by KSTP-TV, Minneapolis, WCCO-TV/CBS News, and by several sports magazines, including *Sports Illustrated*, plus, of course, newspapers throughout the nation.

Minnesota had hired a new varsity basketball coach, Bill Musselman. At Ashland College in Ohio, Musselman's teams had compiled a remarkable 129-30 record, and his 1968-69 team had been voted college divisional champions by both the Associated Press and United Press International. His last five teams at Ashland were rated number one in defense. One of those squads, known as "Musselman's Misers," broke the modern NCAA record, allowing only 33.9 points per game. Musselman even wrote a book about that squad, calling it *33.9 Defense.* That

23

same team also shattered a national record for the fewest personal fouls in a game—ten. When Musselman came to Minnesota, he was the youngest coach in the university's history.

Minnesota basketball had fallen on evil times. Back in 1937 the Gophers had managed to win a share of the Big Ten championship, but thirty-five years is a long time to go without glory. In fact the last time they had won a Big Ten title outright was back in 1919 when basketball was in its relative infancy. Fan interest was on the wane. Musselman seemed to be the answer.

"How long will it take you to turn Minnesota into a winner?" he was asked by the committee which would select a new coach.

"We'll win right off," replied Musselman bluntly. "I don't believe in rebuilding years."

The basketball tenets Musselman lived by were discipline, basic fundamentals, defense, and team unity. He expounded: "Discipline is the most important thing in life, and it holds true for any sport—baseball, football, basketball, or tennis. In basketball it's footwork, ball handling, moving effectively without the ball, timing, shooting technique, defense. All these things are essential for a winning team. Above all, defense. Any team can have cold nights shooting, but if the defense is sound, it can offset this weakness."

When he got the job, Musselman surrounded himself with coaches who believed in his type of basketball. They all shared his basketball philosophy. Their names were Bill Klucas, Jim Williams, and Kevin Wilson.

Klucas, out of Miami University, had won letters in basketball, baseball, football, and track. Williams had been a key player in Musselman's 33.9 defense at Ashland. He had won honorable mention in the small college All-American lists, and also all-tourney honors in the NCAA college division in 1968-69. Wilson had been an All-American guard at Ashland, and a UPI All-American choice during his junior and senior years at Ashland. He shot over 50 percent from the floor and better than 80 percent from the free-throw line. Wilson handled the ball 70 percent of the playing time and averaged less than two turnovers per game. He had been drafted by the Utah Stars of the American Basketball Association, but chose to attend graduate school and become a college coach.

It was Williams who spotted Winfield playing intramural basketball and convinced him to try out for the varsity. It wasn't solely because he thought Dave could make the team, or, if he did, could play regularly. But players were needed who could bolster the starting five and be utilized to spell the varsity five as they were needed. A basketball squad needed twelve to fourteen top-notch players to round out the squad. Some college squads utilized as many as twenty men on the team.

Winfield was under no illusions that he had a chance to be a starter. This was a Minnesota team loaded with talent and he was aware of it. Many on the team would be drafted by the pros after their college careers were over.

Jim Brewer, the captain, was a court magician. He could bring the ball up against the press, dribble like a guard and feed the ball inside. A former member of the United States Olympic team, Brewer had been named Most Valuable Player of the Big Ten. The *Chicago Tribune* called him "Mr. Basketball." In the pro draft, Cleveland's Bill Fitch would trade two starters and a first-round choice to Portland for a crack at Brewer.

Ron Behagen, out of New York's De Witt Clinton High School, had made All-City twice. He was a spectacular forward, capable of shooting with either hand. He averaged 13 rebounds per game. Behagen played with the U.S. Olympic team against the Soviet Union. He would be chosen seventh in the draft by the Kansas City Kings.

Forward Clyde Turner, another Gopher named to the All-Big-Ten team, was a top scorer, averaging 18 points per game. He would be drafted by Milwaukee.

Marvin "Corky" Taylor, who ran on the University's track team, would be drafted by the Boston Celtics, who liked fast men.

For the first part of the season Winfield decorated the bench. Musselman followed the "iron men" theory and expected his players to be on the court most of the forty minutes that comprise a college basketball game. Winfield rooted, fretted, and wondered if the whole thing wasn't a big mistake. At least he saw action with the Soulful Strutters. The big change in his status came after the game against Ohio State on January 25, 1972.

Minnesota had won its first four Big Ten Conference games and Ohio State had won its first three. The players on both teams had reached an emotional high, the Gophers perhaps even more so. Musselman always was a master at psyching up his players. Evidence of his hype was everywhere, as in the sign over the shower room which read, "Defeat is worse than death, because you have to live with defeat."

It was a variation on Vince Lombardi's "winning is everything."

The feeling of tension had communicated itself to the Minnesota fans, all 18,000 of them. When the Ohio State players came out on the floor they were greeted by a thunderous chorus of boos. The Gophers heard cheers that reverberated and filled the arena.

Musselman's pre-game tactics included a routine somewhat similar to that used by the Harlem Globetrotters, with a lot of fancy passing, cute dribbling, and shooting. It was done to the sound of terribly loud, raucous rock music with a wild, driving beat that could be heard and felt in downtown Minneapolis. Musselman said it motivated his players. It also sent the crowd into a frenzy.

Despite the circus atmosphere, the game was mostly clean, hard fought, and tightly officiated. It was only when the half ended that a relatively minor incident occurred, and it proved a harbinger of things to come.

As both teams filed off the court, Minnesota's Bob Nix and State's Luke Witte crossed paths. For whatever reason, Nix raised his arm in a clenched-fist salute. Witte tried to shove Nix's fist away with his elbow and in so doing lightly popped Nix on the jaw. Witte was 7 feet tall, Nix, 6-3.

According to Musselman, "Our kids were really upset by that."

Nevertheless the second half began and continued in the same rough but clean version of college basketball. Soon Behagen fouled out and was replaced by Corky Taylor, whose jump shot with 11:41 remaining gave the Gophers a 32-30 lead. The Buckeyes came roaring back with ten unanswered points to go ahead, 40-32. Minnesota tried hard but couldn't get closer than five points. As defeat loomed, Minnesota fans became more and more unruly, throwing peanuts and partly filled Coke cups onto the floor, making a mess of the court. The game was stopped time and again for quick maintenance and mopping. At one point an announcement was made over the public address system warning the fans that such behavior would result in a technical foul called on the Gophers. The fans responded with boos and more debris.

The situation was a ticking time bomb; even a misinterpreted gesture could have set it off. However, there was no mistaking what happened; it was blatant enough to stun any objective viewer. Here is what was reported by any number of people in the audience that night.

With the Buckeyes ahead, 50-44, and 36 seconds left on the clock, Luke Witte drove to the basket for what should have been an easy layup. Clyde Turner cut in front of Witte and crashed into him. At almost the same instant, Gopher Corky Taylor let go with a long right hook that landed on Witte's ear. That monstrous Minnesota crowd cheered the clobbering and booed when Turner was called for a flagrant foul and ejected from the game.

Witte was on the floor. He rolled over, shaky, and got to all fours. Taylor walked over to him and extended his hand. It looked like a sportsmanlike gesture, one that seemed to say, "Hey, I'm sorry about that." It was no such thing.

As Witte was getting to his feet with the aid of Taylor's pulling hand, Taylor stepped in and gave Witte a knee in the groin. In agony, Witte crashed to the floor, the fans screamed, and the riot was on. Fists flew from all directions.

As Witte lay writhing on the boards, Buckeye guard Dave Merchant went after Taylor. Jim Brewer intercepted him and began throwing bunches of punches; then he and Turner ganged up to chase Merchant along the sidelines. Meanwhile, Behagen left his seat on the bench, ran over to Witte, and began to stomp his face and neck. Behagen was pulled off the helpless Witte.

Next, according to an account of the incident which was published in *Sports Illustrated,* "Dave Winfield, who recently joined the Gopher varsity, joined the fray too, dodging to midcourt where some Minnesota reserves and civilians were trying to wrestle Ohio State substitute Mark Wagar to the floor. Winfield leaped on top of Wagar and hit him five times with his right fist on the face and head."

Stunned, Wagar managed to break free momentarily, but another fan put him on the floor while a different fan punched him on the chin.

27

Eventually some semblance of order was restored. The final seconds of the game were not played.

Witte, bleeding and numb, was taken out of the arena on a stretcher. He remembered almost nothing. "I went blank after I was hit with the knee," he said. "The next thing I knew I was in the emergency room at the hospital."

According to onlookers, Wagar got to his feet and helped Witte off the court. But Wagar has no recollection of doing that.

Patching up Witte was not easy. His left ear and lower lip were swollen. He had a scab on his left cheek. The gash on his chin had to be stitched closed. His right eye was completely covered with a white patch.

The governor of Ohio called the incident "a public mugging."

"It was bush," said the Buckeye coach. "I've never seen anything like it. But what do you expect from a bush outfit?"

Paul Giel, a former Gopher All-American in several sports and now the Minnesota athletic director at Minnesota, visited Buckeye coach Fred Taylor in the locker room to offer his apologies. "I knew it would be emotional," he said to the enraged Taylor, "but I had no idea it would be like this."

Wayne Duke, the Big Ten commissioner, had attended the game and he promptly launched an investigation. He interviewed Musselman, Corky Taylor, Nix, Behagen, and others, he studied films of the game, he listened to conflicting stories and theories, trying to find out why the players and fans had suddenly come unglued.

Some, such as Witte's father, a professor of philosophy, blamed the Minnesota coach. "I'm not surprised," he commented. "Musselman's intent seems to be to win at any cost. His players are brutalized and animalized to achieve that goal."

The same *Sports Illustrated* article noted that Musselman made no attempt to stop the fight and showed no remorse afterward. Then the magazine quoted Ohio State coach Fred Taylor: "There's more at stake here than basketball."

As if to bear out Taylor's thoughts, Ohio State guard Benny Allison suggested racism was at the root of the riot, with the Minnesota blacks against the Ohio State whites. "It was a racial thing," Allison said. "Wardell Jackson and I were right there in the middle of the floor and nobody took a swing at us. They just went for the other guys. Sometimes things like that happen."

Both Allison and Jackson are black.

Corky Taylor claimed the whole mess started when Witte spit at him. Witte replied that he never spit at anybody, and besides, he was down too low to even think of such a thing. Then Taylor told the commissioner he *thought* Witte was going to spit at him.

Commissioner Duke delivered his findings: "The Witte-Nix incident [the raised fist and elbow clip on the chin] resulted from excessive physical contact. There was no evidence of racial overtones. The spitting charges were not substantiated." It all boiled down to Corky Taylor's "unsportsmanlike conduct."

Ron Behagen and Corky Taylor were suspended from basketball competition for the rest of the season.

Duke's decision was not, in the opinion of many, a satisfactory one. The racial aspects seemed to have been swept under the rug as potentially too explosive. And the nagging question remained, why wasn't Dave Winfield also suspended? Winfield himself has never commented on the decision and has long considered the matter closed.

Musselman seemed subdued afterward. He issued new directives to his players. "From now on nobody leaves the bench. Hands go straight up on fouls. Nobody questions the referees. Everything is 'Yes, sir,' 'No, sir.'"

Musselman's wife suffered with him. "I stretched out on the kitchen floor for three days and just wanted to give up," she said.

Behagen and Taylor took their suspensions hard. Taylor couldn't eat for a couple of weeks and Behagen just walked around the campus looking lost. For a while he read law and played piano.

"The game meant everything to me," said Behagen, who had come from the black ghettos of New York. "Now I know it can be taken away from me at any time. I've been up against adversity all my life, it's nothing new. It just has to be overcome."

Eventually, Behagen and Taylor did overcome.

As for Dave Winfield, the suspension of his two teammates proved to be a break for him, for now Musselman had to make him a starter. Perhaps Musselman was ready to give him a shot anyway, because

Winfield was proving with each game that he could deliver. Back at the beginning of December, in a game against Wisconsin, he had come off the bench to score 21 points, second only to Behagen's 22. He received some flattering ink from the press as well as a verbal pat from the coach.

"Dave is a great competitor," Musselman had said. "He's the type who won't fold under pressure; he does everything well and gives us a boost."

Winfield replaced Behagen in the lineup for the first time just four days after the Ohio State game, and during the last eleven games he averaged eleven points and nine rebounds per contest.

Despite the loss of Taylor and Behagen, the Gophers had enough depth—including Winfield—to win the Big Ten basketball title outright for the first time since 1919. But the team couldn't get through the NCAA regionals. Florida State routed them, 70–56, and the season was over.

"Man, I'm glad that's over," Winfield said when he returned home. Then he took his baseball glove off the shelf, packed a bag, and joined the Siebert forces on their annual trip to the warmer climate of Texas.

4

Black Captain—
White Team

As far as Dave Winfield's junior year was concerned the baseball season
was a total washout, at least when he tried playing for the Minnesota
team.

Although he was born and reared in the upper Midwest, where winter
temperatures below zero are the norm, he never cared for cold weather.
The muscles of his body seemed to respond to warmth—he once missed
a bus for a game because he was in the university steam room trying to
loosen up his shoulder muscles. When the time came for him to continue
his baseball career at the university, he couldn't. He was useless to the
team. There was too much pain.

"Dave tried to pitch against Michigan in 30-degree weather," Siebert
said to reporters, "and I think the cold weather did something to his
arm."

Winfield's sore arm also precluded playing in the Metro League again,
but there one baseball opportunity arose and he grabbed it. Fortunately it
is warm in the summertime in Alaska, because the team was in Fairbanks. They were called the Goldpanners.

The Alaska Goldpanners were founded in 1959 by Red Boucher, a former naval aerographer and weatherman. At one time he was the mayor of Fairbanks, a city of some 20,000; he was also executive director of the Fairbanks Industrial Development Corporation. But above all, he loved baseball. That was why he founded the Goldpanners in the first place—to interest the youth of the area in baseball. By the mid-1970s there were some 2,000 boys playing in the area's organized leagues, which ranged from Little League to Senior Babe Ruth Leagues.

Boucher recruited his players from the leading colleges in America, and if his program was not generally known by the rank-and-file baseball fan, it was certainly notable in collegiate circles. Each year he received hundreds of applications. Among those who have played for the Goldpanners over the years are Graig Nettles of the Yankees, Gary Sutherland of the Expos, and such other present or former major leaguers as Mike Gallagher, Mike Adamson, Rick Monday—and Dave Winfield.

Technically, the Goldpanners are a semi-pro team. That is, they receive no money directly for playing baseball, but they are given jobs in the community at salaries of about $700 a month (the pay scale when Winfield played) and are boarded out with families, who consider them "summer sons." The Goldpanners play a non-league schedule, from about mid-June through early August, and their opponents consist of the best college and military teams and other good amateur teams. Home games are in Growder Memorial Park, a pretty good facility considering the area, and attendance hovers in the vicinity of fifty thousand fans per season. By comparison, considering population and seating capacity, a major league team such as Detroit would have to draw close to four million fans to equal Fairbanks' showing.

The team usually is honored with a number of awards, some of them in jest. For instance, the Goldpanners have been named "Best Dressed Team," "Most Popular Team," "Most Aggressive Team," and, to be sure, "Team Traveling the Farthest."

And, once in a while, the Goldpanners can boast of a former player who is undoubtedly destined for the Hall of Fame. Citizens of Fairbanks brag that Tom Seaver once pitched there.

To be sure, there is no All-Star game in Alaska, but to the good burghers of Fairbanks, there is a local contest which is far more colorful and offers more entertainment than anything the major leagues can provide. That is the Midnight Sun Game, which is played on June 21, the date of the summer solstice. On that date there is no night, no artificial lights are needed, and the game gets under way at 10:30 P.M. The pre-game festivities include fireworks, the crowning of Miss Baseball, and Eskimo dances. How can any club beat that?

When Winfield went to Alaska as a pitcher, his arm still wasn't in shape, although he did work sporadically in relief. However, a new facet of his ability suddenly opened up in one game when he was called on to pinch hit with the bases loaded. Dave stepped in on a fastball, got his bat around, and clobbered it out of the park and onto the roof of a bowling alley.

From that moment on he began to play the outfield regularly.

Winfield went on to hit fifteen home runs, lead the Goldpanners in hitting, and be voted Most Valuable Player on the Fairbanks team. Perhaps those brief six or seven weeks in Alaska convinced him that he might do something more than pitch for Minnesota when his senior year rolled around. He could hit good college pitching, and hit with power. Why couldn't he do the same for Minnesota when he wasn't on the mound?

Upon Winfield's return to the university, he sat down with coaches Siebert and Musselman and found awaiting him some good news and some bad news. The good news was that during fall baseball practice, his teammates had elected him captain of the team, replacing Ken Schulz, who had been drafted by the Minnesota Twins. Dave felt it was a signal honor for two reasons: first, he had done absolutely nothing for the team in his junior year, yet they wanted him as their leader. Second, he was the only black player on the squad.

Dave took his role seriously, much to Siebert's delight. "The day after that," the coach said, "I got to the field at 2:30 and he already had the team in the outfield doing calisthenics."

The election pleased Dave more than anything that had happened to him at the university. He was always hungry for respect and admiration. And to be elected captain of one of the strongest teams in the conference, and by a team of all-white players, was without a doubt a magnificent show of the esteem with which his teammates regarded him. It must have given him pause for a moment or two, considering that Dave Winfield, though he made no display of it, was very, very conscious of his race.

Black studies was one of his two majors at Minnesota. "I have my own convictions about things that happen in society," he said, "and I will always make my true feelings known to my people. I don't think you can stick a label like 'militant' on me. I just want to let my people know where I'm coming from, and that I'll be with them, which I always will be. And if I can do any good in any area that concerns black people, I most certainly will. I figure that's my job."

Dave Winfield isn't generally outspoken, but when he speaks, he "tells it like it is."

"It took me awhile to become aware of the fact that I'm a black man in what is basically a white society, a society in which we don't have a full part.

"Every day of your life, someone lets you know you're black," he continues. "You have to deal with it. You can't overlook it. It doesn't matter how much money I'm paid for my work in the future; even if I was to become a millionaire, I'd still be black. There'd still be somebody who would call me a nigger son-of-a-bitch just because of my face."

It might all sound very bitter, but Dave Winfield is not a bitter man. There's a good deal of logic to his thinking, and he says what he's thinking, as objectively as any man could, in a straightforward, unemotional, matter-of-fact way.

"I'm just another brother," he says, "who's trying to make it."

That's evidently how his teammates saw him, too: a brother who was just trying to make it. They weren't intimidated into voting for him as captain of the team; they had been around long enough to know how he felt about being black and all that goes with it: that special sensitivity, resentment, suspicion, even anger. But he was the best man on the team for the job; he had all the qualities that makes a man a leader: courage, determination, the spirit that unifies a team, and the will to win.

The white Minnesota baseball players deserve credit for something that, even these days, is much too rare: the respect, admiration, and acknowledgment of a man's value, whatever the color of his skin or his religion, and the willingness to follow that man as a leader.

But there was bad news as well, and it was given bluntly by Mussel-man. Behagen was back, he would be playing his old position, and Winfield was back as a sixth man. But Dave went out for basketball anyway. He was beginning to enjoy the game more, to relish the one-on-one competition, although his true love remained baseball. In a sense his preference was practical. He had renewed self-confidence in his baseball ability after performing so well in Alaska, and he knew he had an excellent chance of sticking around for a long time in the big leagues. In basketball, however, he still had a long way to go. As he put it, "There are a lot of basketball superstars around, and at this point I can't see myself going against a guy like Kareem Abdul Jabbar."

Winfield did start the season on the bench, but as the season pro-gressed he found himself on the court with increasing frequency. And when he was playing, Winfield made every minute count. Against Iowa he scored 14 points, making good on seven baskets out of ten shots. He started against Michigan State and Minnesota won, 93-77, with Winfield hitting four of eight shots and taking down six rebounds.

Where Winfield got the energy to play so solidly was a mystery, because starting in February of that year he took a baseball workout before basketball three times a week. Musselman didn't object, knowing how much baseball meant to him. And Dave wanted no repetition of his sore arm, so he threw for forty-five minutes during his workouts.

Interest in Winfield mounted as the season progressed, even when the Gophers lost. In a late February game against Michigan, Winfield had ten points and seven rebounds in the first half. But he scored only one more field goal in the game—it turned out to be the sole bucket the Gophers got in the first nine minutes of the second half, as the Wolver-ines went on to win, 64-52. Winfield was the team's leading scorer with 15 points and the leading rebounder with 14.

"It was as good an inside game as anyone has played for us this year," said coach Musselman. "One of the things that went wrong for us in the second half was that we couldn't get the ball to him. In the first half he made some shots I've never even seen him take in practice."

Winfield's efforts, as much as anyone else's, helped the Gophers get into the National Invitational Tournament, but there was trouble in paradise as the baseball schedule loomed on the horizon. Siebert's men were scheduled to go to Texas again for the spring opener against St. Mary's University on March 23. The finals of the NIT were set for March 25.

Speaking about the dilemma, Winfield said candidly, "I talked to coach Siebert and he thinks it would be for my own good to go south with the baseball team. [Winfield did *not* mention the obvious fact that he was captain of the team.] I would like to go to Texas and get the benefit of the warm weather and sunshine. I'm behind in my pitching now."

Again the specter of his sore arm was haunting him. Any recurrence during his last shot as a senior would be a disaster. No big league club shells out the heavy money for a sore-armed pitcher.

There is no doubt that at that particular moment Dave Winfield was a man torn apart; the image he presented was blurred by equal parts of immaturity, sensitivity, and sincerity. He reveled in two nicknames he himself fostered, one being "Dave the Rave," the other, "the D.S.— Designated Superman." Perhaps they were an oblique reference to his popularity with the young ladies on campus, which was understandable enough since he was, after all, a tall, strong, good-looking young man with fine prospects for the future. Still, that isn't exactly the modest, All-American figure the public likes to admire as a shining example of a clean-cut American athlete.

And, as good as he was on the court, he seemed to be missing some ingredient—call it the spark of true greatness and dedication. Even Musselman, who had heaped praise on Winfield, said of him, "He played like baseball was his number-one sport."

His teammates, at times, felt as Musselman did. An article in the Sunday magazine section of *The New York Times,* written by respected author Phil Berger, shed new and surprising light on Winfield's basketball career during his senior season. Berger wrote of the way his teammates treated Winfield and how he was defended by assistant coach Jim Williams: "Others on the squad, intent on pro careers, saw Winfield as a threat to their ambitions. 'And what happened,' said Williams, 'was that they tried to mess him up, calling him "that baseball player," saying he shouldn't be starting, accusing him of shooting the ball too much, picking on him for no good reason.'

"One afternoon," the article continued, "during a practice drill, Winfield suddenly stopped running and, with tears in his eyes, dropped to one knee. 'He was,' said Williams, 'used to being appreciated in baseball. He wanted to be liked here, too, and was not. It kind of bothered him.' "

Berger concluded, "Winfield did not give in to hostile teammates. At one practice he and teammate Ron Behagen, who later played professional basketball, came to blows, and Winfield—according to coach Williams—got the better of it. From then on the pressure abated.

" 'I'm easygoing,' said Winfield, remembering the incident, 'but if something's unjust, all I can say is, watch out!' "

The basketball-vs.-baseball conflict faded away when Minnesota's team was quickly eliminated in the NIT. Winfield turned his full attention to baseball—well, *almost* his full attention. He was also fooling around in intramural track, where the best high jump was about 6 feet. Winfield took a few practice jumps in stocking feet, wearing his baseball warmup jacket. He jumped an estimated 6 feet 7 inches. That made him the intramural champ, at least for the moment.

Minnesota won the Big Ten baseball title again. Dave Winfield made sure they did, providing leadership and inspiration. Games ended quickly when Dave was in good form and had good support. One big success was the doubleheader against hapless Augsburg, which the Gophers won, 18-1 and 21-0. Winfield pitched only five innings of the opener since there was no sense working hard against a team that offered little more than an afternoon's workout. Dave struck out five, walked three, and got three hits in as many at-bats; one hit was a three-run homer over the left-center fence.

Other games were a struggle. The Gophers were losing to Northwestern, 6-1 in the ninth. The game ended with Minnesota winning, 8-6, thanks to a two-run homer by Winfield. In an earlier game, trailing Illinois by 6-3 in the final inning, Winfield and his Gophers battled back to pull it out, 7-6.

In the regional tournament Winfield hurled a sparkling 13-strikeout, six-hit shutout against Southern Illinois as the Gophers won, 2-0. Then came a grueling duel against All-American Jackson Todd and the University of Oklahoma Sooners.

For seven innings both pitchers pitched shutout ball. In the bottom of the eighth the Gophers got the leadoff man on base only to have him erased in a double play. Then three consecutive singles by Bruce Nordquist, Joe Comer, and Tim Grice put a run across. Minnesota took the field in the top of the ninth clinging to a precarious 1-0 lead.

Dave wasn't out of the woods yet. Clawing their way back, the Sooners loaded the bases with one out. But Dave hitched up his pants, bowed his neck and struck out the next two batters, both going down on 3-and-2 pitches. They were his 13th and 14th strikeout victims of the game.

But Minnesota couldn't win the big one against the Trojans of Southern California, although Dave Winfield pitched his heart out for eight innings. By then the Gophers had the Trojans down, 7-0. Winfield had struck out 15 and allowed only one infield hit so far. But he had completely run out of gas. Going into the ninth inning he had already thrown 165 pitches and he tried hard to close it out. He almost did.

USC got to Winfield for two singles with one out, and Trojan Fred Lynn (who later starred with Boston before being dealt to California) grounded one along the first-base line. Gopher first baseman Chris Brown messed it up, threw to the plate and the catcher dropped the ball. Two runs scored. Another single scored run number three and finished Winfield.

Southern Cal never faltered. Gopher relief pitcher Bob Turnbull permitted three singles, and the catcher was charged with two passed balls. Three more runs scored, and Gordon Peterson came to the mound. The only out he got was a run-scoring sacrifice fly. The Trojans wrapped it up, 8-7.

But by then Winfield had known for a couple of weeks that he had been drafted by the San Diego Padres, the fourth player chosen in the annual amateur draft. Pro basketball was also after him; Dave had been selected by the Atlanta Hawks of the National Basketball Association and the Utah Stars of the American Basketball Association. Oddly enough, although he had never set foot on a college gridiron, Winfield was also selected by the Minnesota Vikings of the National Football League. Evidently they thought that with his 6 feet 6 inches and 225 pounds, he had the makings of a tight end.

Winfield's stats in his senior year were simply unbelievable. His pitching record was 9-1, with a 2.74 earned run average. In 82 innings he allowed 64 hits and 25 earned runs, walking 40 and striking out 109.

Playing the outfield when he wasn't pitching, Winfield got into 43 games and hit for a .385 average, including eight home runs and 33 runs batted in. His fielding was outstanding; he made only two errors all year.

In spite of his superb record, Winfield had his detractors. Max Nichols, sports editor of the *Minneapolis Star,* wrote a provocative column taking Winfield to task. Nichols praised Winfield's athletic talent and the way he made good through his own efforts, climbing from a St. Paul playground to national prominence. Then he let the Gopher athlete have it: "I don't like his attitude so far, the way he has put personal ambitions ahead of his team on at least two occasions. And I question whether he will make it as a professional star in either basketball or baseball unless he learns to put his team ahead of himself."

Nichols cited his tremendous pitching in the NCAA tournament and his play on the basketball team, but two incidents nagged at him. One concerned the NIT. Minnesota had lost much prestige by dropping the last two regular season games to Iowa and Northwestern.

"But Winfield decided to go south with the baseball team because he felt his personal chances of signing a professional contract probably would be better in baseball," Nichols wrote. "Then, after he was convinced that he would be seen by the top professional basketball scouts during the NIT in New York, he changed his mind and stayed with the basketball team."

The other incident that bothered Nichols was Winfield's complaint to coach Siebert that he had not been touted enough to reporters. "He disregarded the effect this might have had on the Gophers in the district tourney."

Thus Nichols voiced doubts about Winfield's statements that he was really a team player. He readily conceded Winfield's talent but questioned his willingness to be part of a unit. His parting shot was, "Big money offers now will not insure Winfield's ultimate success."

Actually, Dave Winfield's ultimate success later insured the big money offers, but he would be challenged in the media time and again by those questioning the very things he was also being praised for.

5

On the Team that Hamburgers Bought

When Dave Winfield rejoined the San Diego Padres in 1974 for his first full season in the majors, several drastic changes had already been made. The club had been sold to Ray Kroc, the hamburger mogul, a deal that probably forestalled shifting the franchise to Washington, D.C. The Padres and San Diego fans had become disenchanted with each other. Some Padres fans joked that the team had been in the cellar so long it had started to grow roots.

Washington, on the other hand, was accustomed to finishing at the bottom of the heap. The nation's capital had fielded an American League team twice before, and each time the club had been met with an unusual display of public apathy. For many years, regardless of which version of the team was at hand, the press referred to Washington as "first in war, first in peace, and last in the American League."

Ray Kroc had been around. During World War I, when he was fifteen years old, he lied about his age and became a member of the ambulance corps when the United States became embroiled in the conflict. Later he played piano in traveling bands and got a job as musical director for a radio station in Chicago. In those days musical directors often strayed from their designated chores and Kroc hired an act called "Sam 'n' Henry," which ultimately became "Amos 'n' Andy," the most popular radio show of its era.

Kroc was a baseball fan, a die-hard Chicago Cubs rooter. He was also a terrific salesman, an outstanding sales manager, and a fantastic organizer. He began selling for the Lili-Tulip Cup Corporation, and then he took over exclusive sales for the milkshake multimixer machine, a new invention. A small hamburger restaurant in San Bernardino, California, owned by the McDonald brothers, bought eight machines.

The year was 1954, Ray Kroc was 52 years old, and he celebrated his birthday by buying out the McDonald brothers. He then began to develop the idea of a franchise system. He was in such financial straits at this time that he offered his secretary a percentage of the company if she would work for nothing. She agreed and within five years was able to retire with a net worth of about $60 million. There were others who made millions, particularly when McDonald's went public. Today with more than 5,000 outlets around the world, and a slogan, "You deserve a break today," the chain has become a national institution, and Kroc's fortune is estimated at about $500 million.

For years Kroc tried to buy his favorite team, the Cubs, but Mr. Phil Wrigley would not let go. He could have bought the White Sox, but Kroc says: "I'm strictly a National Leaguer. How could I grow up following the National League all of my life and then wind up owning an American League team?"

Kroc's first move was to get his Padres out of their old, yellow, tired-looking uniforms, which, Don Freeman said, made the players look like "prancing dandelions," and dress them in snappy white, with yellow and blue stripes along the pants. More important, he had his checkbook open and ready to deal for players who could contribute to the team.

Kroc made his first big mistake when he turned the Padres into a family business. His wife, Joan, sat on the board of directors. His son-in-law, Ballard Smith, was made president of the organization. Ray Kroc, in all his wisdom, knew how to promote and market quick lunches, but he had yet to learn there was a vast difference between the hamburger and baseball industries. The Padres were going nowhere when he acquired their assets. By the end of the decade their destination remained unchanged.

As we shall see, over the years Kroc would let some quality players slip away for one reason or another. He would get rid of Dave Kingman because, as he put it, "He was a slob, and because he didn't run to and from the dugout and his position in left field." George Hendrick was to be sent away, reportedly because he failed to show up at a dinner in Kroc's honor. The Padres had a chance to sign a bright young third-base prospect named Doug DeCinces, but general manager Buzzy Bavasi offered $4,000 and DeCinces wanted $6,000. Oscar Gamble, an authentic long-ball threat, was on the roster but would be dealt to the Texas Rangers. Jerry Mumphrey would play a lot of center field for the Padres, but in his option year, coming off a good season and wanting a great amount of money to sign again, Mumphrey would go to the Yankees.

There was a new manager as well as a fresh owner. His name was John McNamara. Like other successful managers, such as Joe McCarthy of the Yankees and Walt Alston of the Dodgers, McNamara had only an arm's-length acquaintance with baseball as a major league player.

McNamara, a quiet, personable man broke into baseball as a catcher and never rose above Triple A. Mostly he remained in the middle minors with the kind of statistics that would never threaten or even approach a .300 batting average. But he knew the game from a managerial stand-point, and he showed it when he won back-to-back pennants in the Southern League in 1966 with Mobile and in 1967 with Birmingham. His next stop was a coaching job with the Oakland Athletics, and he managed during the last 13 games of the season when Hank Bauer stepped down. The following season he guided the A's to a second-place finish for the second time in as many years. As a reward Charley Finley bade him farewell, which was par for the course with Finley. From 1971 through 1973 McNamara coached the San Francisco Giants, and now he had turned up at the helm in San Diego.

If Dave Winfield was bewildered by the antics of his new boss, he had every right to be. On opening day of 1974 a goodly crowd was on hand at Jack Murphy Stadium, behaving like born-again Californians, believing that they were going to have a winner now that a man with an open wallet was in charge. Kroc, an instant folk hero, played to the throng like he was leading a revival meeting. Introduced over the PA system, beaming at the crowd's standing ovation, the Big Mac magnate lifted his hands to them in benediction.

"With your help and God's help," he intoned into the PA system, "we'll raise hell tonight."

And raise hell he did, but not with the fans. The club was under new management, but Kroc was still peddling the same old losses. A thick layer of gloom settled over the crowd, and by the eighth inning the Padres were down, 9-5. It was then that Kroc walked into the public address booth and picked up the microphone.

"Ladies and gentlemen," he said, "I suffer with you." Amid gasps and cheers he continued, "The good news is that you loyal San Diego fans have outstripped Los Angeles. They had 31,000 on opening night, we have 40,000."

The cheers increased as the crowd indulged in self-congratulations for showing up. Just then a completely naked man came out of nowhere and ran to second base. The streaker touched the bag, then raced to right field and disappeared into the stands. The fans were convulsed with laughter, but Mr. Kroc was not amused.

"Get him out of here!" he hollered over the PA system. "Take him to jail!"

The fans broke up completely. Shouts of derision and resentment mingled with snorts of utter frustration. Kroc wasn't finished yet. He had to leave a parting shot of contempt for his baseball team.

He snarled into the PA system, "The bad news is, I've never seen such stupid ball playing in my life!"

Kroc's words were not well received by the Padres or by their opponents, the Houston Astros. Willie McCovey, the venerable slugger playing his first game with the Padres, said, "We may have played sloppy but we're professionals and we know when the hell we play that way. We don't have to be reminded."

Doug Rader of the Astros chipped in, "What does he think we are, short order cooks or something?"

Marvin Miller, head of the Baseball Players Association, remarked, "The players of the San Diego Padres and Houston Astros have demonstrated by their restraint in the face of Mr. Kroc's insults that their intelligence far exceeds his."

Chub Feeney, president of the National League, was also unhappy. He issued an edict that limited the use of the public address system in any ball park to the control of the PA announcer, making it off limits for everyone else. Bowie Kuhn, commissioner of baseball, demanded that Kroc apologize immediately.

Kroc did apologize. He said, "What I regret now is using the word 'stupid.' People who know me realize that I meant it, but not in the dictionary sense. I meant it in the sense of, 'Okay, we made a stupid move, now let's smarten up.' I'm a bohunk and that's the way I talk."

The Padres that year were a mixture of over-the-hill veterans and kids who might not have been quite ready to do battle with the rest of the National League West.

The star of the Padres was Willie McCovey, and, of course, once he joined the team he was called "Big Mac." Willie was a proven superstar, whose mere presence in the lineup provided the Padres with the home-run potential the team had always lacked. His mere presence gave the team stature, and he was the first big drawing card the team had ever had. Willie came to the Padres in 1974 after fifteen star-studded seasons with the Giants, where he powered the ball for some 415 home runs. In 1963, Willie slugged out 44 homers; in 1965 he drove out 39 home runs, then followed in 1966 with 36. In 1969, Willie slugged 45 home runs. He still was a fearsome sight at the plate, hunching his six-foot-six body behind one of the most vicious batting swings in baseball, and even though he was 36 years old and bothered by sore knees, he carried a constant threat of hitting the ball out of the park.

Nate Colbert was another slugger on the team. Nate drove out 38 home runs for the Padres in 1970, then followed with 27 homers in 1971, and 38 homers in 1972.

There were other and rather ordinary players, such as Enzo Hernandez, a slick shortstop from Venezuela; rookie pitchers Larry Hardy and Dave Feeisleben; catcher Fred Kendall; and Derrel Thomas at second base. But the best of the younger players was Dave Winfield, whose total major league experience added up to exactly 56 games.

For both Winfield and the Padres, 1974 was an up-and-down season.

Both would go through hot streaks, then cool off. Occasionally, Mc-Namara would bench Dave, and perhaps the rest would be beneficial, because he would come back swinging. But he was still an unknown quantity that year; the recognition he craved eluded him. An incident that summer was indicative of his status in the National League.

With a girl on his arm, Winfield entered a department store where future Hall of Famer Bob Gibson was autographing copies of his book. Dave approached the pitcher casually.

"Hello, Mr. Gibson," he said. "Do you know who I am?"

Gibson responded with a noncommittal grunt which Winfield took as a form of a rebuff. Dave made a mental note that Gibson would recognize him the next time they met.

Two weeks later, playing the Cardinals, Dave faced Gibson. The big righthander struck him out with a low, outside slider.

"I went back to the bench and I was really hot," said Winfield afterward. "I told Cito Gaston and Nate Colbert that I was going to take Hoot Gibson out of the yard my next time up."

Dave was looking for the slider. When it came he hammered it over the left-center fence, to insure a 3-1 win for the Padres.

"Gibson watched me all the way around the bases," Dave said. "He remembered who I was."

There was a similar episode when Winfield encountered Willie Mays. "I introduced myself to him," Dave recalled, "and he asked me if I was an outfielder or a pitcher." Unfortunately, there was no way he could get back at Mays for that. Although he was not depressed, Dave did not hide his unhappiness.

"Two of my idols," he said ruefully. "I finally got to meet them and it was a real letdown. After all those years of idolizing those great stars."

Yet all was not sour for Winfield. There were times when he felt it was great to be alive, to be a big league baseball player, and to have his God-given talent. One such time was when his father flew down from Seattle to watch him play. From time to time Frank Winfield had watched his son play college ball, and the relationship between them was improving.

"I heard you hit a home run the other night," Frank said to his son upon his arrival at the ballpark. "Too bad I wasn't there."

"That's okay," Dave replied. "I'll hit another one for you tonight."

He did. It was the only run of the game as the Padres beat St. Louis, 1-0.

After the final out, Frank Winfield strutted around the San Diego dressing room with his chest puffed out. "A lot of parents dream of moments like this, and now I'm experiencing one," he said to one and all. "I never thought anything like this would happen. No matter how good your son is, the percentage of kids who reach the big leagues is so small. I'm mighty proud of Dave."

In part Dave's batting inconsistency was due to that persistent hitch in his swing. It was mental to a degree, but the mechanics of his swing were faulty too. Winfield was not above asking for help, and on one occasion he went directly to Lew Fonseca, the Chicago Cubs' batting coach. Without pussyfooting he asked Fonseca for a few batting tips.

"I can't turn him down if he asks me," Fonseca said. "The kid has one good thing going for him, he's got good wrist action, good bat speed. But he has that hitch in his swing. He carries the bat high and then brings it down. If he has to go back up, he can't do it in time. After all, you have only a split second to adjust to a pitch."

The night he talked with Fonseca, Winfield beat the Cubs with a home run. Asked whether Fonseca deserved some of the credit for that homer, Winfield laughed.

"No," he said. "I don't think he helped me that much, not in just one day. It's going to take longer than that. He just told me some of his theories. Lew Fonseca knows what he's doing."

Also, perhaps the words of *Minneapolis Star* sports writer Max Nichols were beginning to sink in. Nichols had written a column taking Winfield to task in his senior year at the university, pointing out that Dave was not, in his opinion, a team player. In a game against the New York Mets, Winfield received a lesson in teamwork that he never forgot.

Willie McCovey batted ahead of Winfield in the lineup. Knowing that he was a dead-pull hitter, the Mets overshifted to the right side, leaving most of the shortstop territory and all of third base unguarded. Knowing that Winfield was swinging a hot bat, McCovey dropped a perfect bunt and beat it out easily for a base hit.

"I had to smile when I saw him lay down that bunt," Winfield said. "I

47

thought, hey, that's real smart. It makes so much sense. The Mets were all on one side of the field, so he bunted to the other side."

McCovey and Winfield were two of the very few bright spots in the San Diego lineup in 1974, as a July 22nd headline indicated. McCovey got the top spot with his pair of home runs, but the subhead read, "Winfield's Hits Help Sink Mets." Big Dave had driven in three runs with a single and a double. At the end of the season McCovey had won the team home-run derby with 22, while Winfield was not far behind with 20.

McNamara said of his young outfielder, "I managed Reggie Jackson at Binghamton at the same stage of his career, and Dave is right now at a comparable level of ability."

Dave's stats did not quite bear out the manager's words. His .265 average in 145 games was no harbinger of future stardom, and some of his 18 doubles were listed as extra-base hits because Winfield's long legs and surprising bursts of speed hustled them out of the singles category. Besides, he struck out 96 times in 498 official at-bats, almost a one-in-five average. He was still overswinging.

Yet Winfield's confidence in himself never flagged. At the beginning of the 1975 spring training session he made all sorts of predictions, that he might hit .300, that 30 home runs might be an attainable goal with close to 100 RBIs. After one and a half years, he felt that he was finally getting the hang of major league baseball.

Whether Winfield could have made good his boast became a moot question early in June. He had started the season with a rush, and by the end of April was batting .338 with six home runs. The Padres ran off nine victories in their first 13 games, one of which was a beautiful six-hit shutout of the Astros, the handiwork of a kid pitcher named Randy Jones. In a May series against Atlanta, another youngster named Mike Ivie went 8-for-12, while Winfield hit home runs in each of the three games. San Diego was playing exciting ball and seemed headed for first place in the National League West. The Padres fans were turning out for home games in record numbers.

Of course it was all an illusion. The Padres were not that good, and they proved it by finishing fourth in their division, 37 games out of first place. Winfield was the victim of misfortune, starting on June 12th.

The Padres had already begun to tail off when they took on the Montreal Expos. Winfield had begun to assess his goals more realistically, especially the 100 RBIs target. The Padres weren't getting on base ahead of him and there were few runs he could have knocked across the plate. He said with a sigh, "I think driving in 100 runs is pretty tough to do."

Still giving it the old college try, Winfield had gone barreling into second base to break up a double play, and his slide sent Expo shortstop Tim Foli flying. Foli, a very aggressive type, bided his time, and had an opportunity to repay Winfield soon enough. In the same situation in a later inning, Dave went toward the bag to disrupt another possible twin kill. Foli took the throw and snapped his relay toward first with an underhand flip that was a trifle low. As Dave was hitting the dirt he saw the ball come at his head and threw up his right hand to protect himself. The ball hit his right wrist and left it numb. Dave, who had been batting .295 at the time, was out of action for 11 games. San Diego lost 7 of them.

Winfield's timing was off when he returned to the lineup, but just as he was starting to groove his swing again, he was hit on the left wrist by a pitched ball in a July 1st game against Los Angeles. The incident precipitated a brawl, which was no way to heal a wrist. Winfield remained in the lineup but could only play with both wrists taped.

The season that had begun so promisingly ended dismally, although the Padres did climb out of the cellar. San Diego was last in both leagues in runs scored, next to last in home runs. The team had made more errors than any other in the majors, allowing more than 100 unearned runs.

As for Winfield, he batted .267 and his home-run output dropped to 15. But he stole 23 bases, in itself no mean feat.

"I could have stolen a lot more," Dave said, "but you don't take a chance on being out at second and erased from the base paths when your team is three, four, or five runs behind in a game."

If there was blame to be assigned for the Padres' relatively poor showing, the culprits were in the front office. Granted there were injuries to key players, but almost every club in both leagues could point to one or more missing stars at some point in the season; that was part of the game. In the main it was the collapse of the San Diego pitching staff and the failure of the front office to remedy the situation that lowered the boom on the team.

The skid started when Alan Foster, obtained through a trade with the Cardinals, developed arm problems. At the time Foster was 4-2; the season was perhaps one-third gone and a replacement for Foster was in order. The Padres, however, were lulled into a false sense of security because at the time the pitching staff was leading the league in earned-run percentage. It was believed that the staff could function with nine pitchers instead of the usual ten. They couldn't. Before long the staff rated sixth in the league.

Only after midseason did the front office listen to the pleas of pitching coach Tom Morgan, and then lefty Brent Strom was called up from Hawaii. Strom did well for a while; then he too came up with a shoulder problem and was sidelined. Again Morgan asked for a replacement, which was not forthcoming. The eventual skid was inevitable.

To the Padres' credit, they did not fire McNamara for a situation obviously not of his making, but coach Tom Morgan was fired.

For many skeptics, the jury on Dave Winfield was still out. He had played two and a half seasons of big league baseball, and after arriving with much fanfare as a potential savior, he had yet to live up to expectations. Sure, he was improving, but that was due to added experience, not the emergence of natural talent. There was no question that he had all the ability—he had just never put the complete act together. The arm was there, the potential power and the fielding, plus more sheer hustle and spirit than a squad of cheerleaders, but for one reason or another the end result seemed to fall short.

6

Making It

San Diego finished in fourth place in the Western Division of the National League, but John McNamara, who had done a very good job with the material at hand, was rehired to manage the club in 1976. It was going to be a better club in '76. For one thing, in the last month of 1975, the Padres acquired Doug Rader from the Houston Astros. Rader had been a Gold Glove winner as a member of *The Sporting News* All-Star fielding teams five of his last six seasons. He was to bring more than his glove to the San Diego Padres.

The 31-year-old Rader could hit with power. He had averaged 24 home runs a season in his nine years with the Astros. He liked to play for a winner. He wasn't the kind of player who haggled over a contract; he wanted the thing signed so he could get into the business of playing third base as quickly as possible. He had an infectious optimism as well.

"If they see an old gaffer like me," he was speaking of himself and the Padres, "playing when they know he's hurting, maybe it will rub off on them."

Rader was known as a bit of a "flake" among the ballplayers in the

51

league, a well-liked "flake," and he figured this "flakiness" ought to help his new teammates in San Diego get "loose."

"Guys who are loose," he said, "are usually very fierce competitors."

The Padres also picked up hard-hitting centerfielder Willie Davis, who was an outstanding player with the Dodgers during a 14-year period. Willie had been traded to Texas and then to the Cardinals, where he hit .291 and drove out 11 home runs in 1975. There were also great expectations for Randy Jones, the Padres' star pitcher who had won 20 games for them in 1975. That was an amazing performance for a club that had won only 71 games all season, against 91 losses, and that finished fourth in a field of six in the National League's Western Division.

Another important acquisition for the 1976 season was Roger Craig, as pitching coach. Craig had pitched for the pennant-winning Brooklyn Dodgers back in 1955, his first year in major league ball, winning the five games that meant the pennant. In that same rookie year, he pitched and won a game for the Dodgers in the World Series. He was a mainstay on the Dodgers' pitching staff, both in Brooklyn and Los Angeles, through 1961. Then he went east again to head the pitching staff of the New York Mets in their first year as an expansion team. Later, he pitched for the St. Louis Cardinals, the Cincinnati Reds, and the Philadelphia Phillies.

After he hung up his glove, he served as a scout, then managed the Albuquerque club to a second-place finish in the Western Division of the Texas League. He was the pitching coach with the Padres from 1969 to early in 1973, went over to the Dodgers, where he served as their minor league pitching instructor, joined the Houston Astros in 1974, and was now back again with the Padres—who could use all his experience and knowledge for their less than brilliant pitching staff. (Craig was to manage the Padres within another season.)

And then, of course, there was David Mark Winfield back on the roster, after signing a new contract with a sizable increase in his paycheck.

At least a month before spring training he was thinking back to the '75 season and planning for '76.

"I had hoped," he said, "last year was going to be my year. But things didn't work out the way I expected, so now I'm pointing to the season coming up.

"I'm not setting any specific goals just yet," he continued. "Let's just say that I'm really looking forward to spring training and having the kind of year I'm capable of."

When reminded of the relay throw that Tim Foli tossed, hitting Dave on the wrist and putting him out of action, he said, "I think it was intentional. I think Tim Foli meant to get me, just like Hough's duster, the one that got the other wrist in Los Angeles, was intentional."

Was he bitter about it?

"I have no animosity in my heart or mind," he answered. "I'm simply looking at the first two months of last season as indicating what I'm capable of doing when I'm healthy. As for injuries, they're a part of the game I hope to avoid."

A lot of thought, and more self-evaluation: "The problem was that I tried to come back too soon after getting hurt. I never did recover completely. I don't think I hit much better than .220 the last four months of the season. I know that I'm a lot better hitter than a .220."

Dave was as happy as any other Padre that Willie Davis and Doug Rader were coming to San Diego—happier. He needed men who could swing the bat in the lineup, to get up to the plate just before him or just after him.

"In our lineup," he protested, "I'm virtually naked. No one behind me and no one in front of me, to score runs or to drive me home.

"I've hit 35 home runs in the past two years, and 30 of them have come with the bases empty. And I'm hitting clean-up. That doesn't make any kind of sense, does it?

"Things should be better with men like Willie Davis, Willie McCovey, and Doug Rader in the lineup," he concluded.

And as usual Dave got off to a fast start almost as soon as he limbered up in the spring of 1976. The ball seemed to jump off his bat, although he swore he wasn't swinging for distance.

"I'm not trying to hit homers," he assured the press gravely, after one Grapefruit League game that showed his power. "Can I help it if three of my singles carried all the way to the fence?"

By the end of March, as Winfield was rounding into shape, he seemed finally to have achieved his niche as a hitter. He told reporters wistfully, "I wouldn't mind a bit if the season started tomorrow. I've always started fast, and what I'd like to do is maintain that fast pace all the way through October."

When the bell rang to open the 1976 season, Winfield's "fast start" had turned into an all-out sprint. A crowd of almost 53,000 attended the opening game in Los Angeles, the largest opening day crowd in Dodger history. Dave's grand slam powered the Padres to victory. It was not only Winfield's first grand slam, it was also his first homer in Los Angeles. The next day he hit another one for all the bases as Randy Jones beat Don Sutton, 3-1.

In their first five games, San Diego scored 21 runs. Dave Winfield drove in 8 of them.

Dave's bat was not the only weapon in his developing arsenal. He had become a go-for-broke fielder, leaping against walls to grab long drives, diving for sinking liners, and throwing bullets to the infield. Base runners were learning to respect his arm; they took few liberties. Although it might be termed heresy to compare some of his moves with those of Joe DiMaggio, there were certain similarities that could not be overlooked, such as his long, loping gait when going after fly balls. He did not seem to be hurrying—indeed, his pace seemed almost leisurely— but he was there when the ball came down and his glove was in place for the catch. Winfield seemed to be emerging as the complete ball player.

"I'm growing in confidence and accomplishments," Dave said, somewhat immodestly, but with reason. "I'm just giving people a glimpse of what I'm going to do in the future. For me these are merely the preliminaries."

In a 5-3 win over St. Louis, Winfield set up a run with a bunt single, and later saved the game with a diving catch of a vicious liner, cutting off two ninth-inning runs that would have beaten the Padres.

He hit a home run against Montreal and set up the winning rally with an infield hit and a stolen base.

He hit a two-run homer in a 4-0 win against the New York Mets and stopped Tom Seaver's streak of eight straight victories over the Padres. By the end of May, Winfield was leading the Padres in runs scored, home runs, runs batted in, walks, and stolen bases.

Yet there were pitchers in the National League who were convinced that Winfield was hitting beyond his abilities, that he could not maintain that pace very long. As the season went into June, the opposing pitchers began to pitch around Willie McCovey, who was batting ahead of Dave, in order to get at Winfield. For the tall outfielder, this was a bonanza. In the past he had complained that there was no one on base for him to drive in. Now he would have at least one in McCovey, and possibly more.

The first time that happened was in Cincinnati. McCovey was walked to load the bases. Dave drove into a fast ball and deposited it into the stands for a grand slam.

The Pittsburgh Pirates were the next crew of unbelievers. History repeated itself. McCovey was passed and Winfield slugged another game-winning homer.

The New York Mets fared no better. McCovey and Enzo Hernandez walked. Winfield belted a home run off veteran pitcher Skip Lockwood.

Winfield was pleased enough about his performance, but he was unhappy over the way the All-Star balloting was progressing. His name did not appear, and he thought, with good reason, that he belonged on the team. Yet he didn't lose heart.

"I still think that if I continue to play as well as I've been playing, I've got a good chance of making the team," he said. Knowing how players were often selected he added, "We're in a small town. The ballot usually falls in favor of the guys playing the big cities. But the coaches do some choosing too. Maybe I'll be going to the All-Star game yet."

Cincinnati's Sparky Anderson, for one, thought Winfield belonged. "He's the finest right fielder in the National League," Sparky said flatly.

In late June Winfield put on an exhibition that seemed to bear out Anderson's words. After the game was over, San Diego's third baseman, Ted Kubiak, said exuberantly, "Everybody talks about how great Reggie Jackson is, but Dave Winfield is a better player."

In the second inning Dave bounced a checked-swing roller toward third and beat the throw for an infield hit. The hit helped develop the first run of the game for the Padres.

In the fourth inning, Dave's routine grounder took a bad hop over shortstop Chris Speier's head. Dave turned on the steam, rounded first, and beat center fielder Larry Herndon's throw to second with a headlong slide. He came around on a single by Hector Torres.

In the eighth, Winfield singled, raced from first to third on an infield out, and scored when Darrel Evans threw wild to third trying to nail him.

"I've said all along that Winfield can become one of the most exciting men ever to play the game," said the beaming McNamara.

Chris Speier merely said, "Winfield stole the game from us." He shook his head in grudging approval and went on, "Winfield is the kind of player who can dominate a game."

Perhaps he could, often enough. But not always. Winfield had his failures, such as the August game against the Mets. In the eighth, with the Padres down, 2-1, they had the tying run on third and the go-ahead run on first with nobody out. Winfield faced Skip Lockwood, the pitcher he had taken downtown earlier in the season. Winfield swung futilely at two bad pitches, then looked at strike three. Tito Fuentes and pinch hitter Willie McCovey also struck out.

McNamara, who had been quick to praise Dave when Winfield merited it, did not hesitate to tell it like it was when his prize outfielder couldn't cut it. "If Dave doesn't swing at the first two pitches, he's got Lockwood in the hole, 2-0," the San Diego skipper said. "The only strike Lockwood threw him was when he struck out."

For Dave Winfield, 1976 was something of a mixed bag. He batted .283, his highest so far in the majors, and his 139 hits were another personal high, as were his 26 stolen bases. But his home-run total dropped to 13.

All his statistics might have been better but for an injury sustained on September 5th that curtailed the season for Winfield. Undoubtedly he would have added a few more RBIs, a home run or two, and perhaps some batting-average points as well. Instead he missed 25 games.

Winfield did not play in that All-Star game, and he made no effort to hide his disappointment. But there would be other years to play in the midsummer classic, and he would make his presence felt. His career had barely begun, and already he was being talked of as a star whose time had come.

Also, along the way, he had met a man named Albert S. Frohman, who was to change his entire life. It was Frohman who would turn Winfield into an instant millionaire.

7

The Benefactor

The year 1977 began with an off-the-field story that made headlines in the St. Paul, Minnesota, newspapers. In mid-February that year, the Padres' star outfielder, Dave Winfield, established the Dave Winfield Outstanding Minority Student-Athlete Awards for the Twin Cities. It was a $1,000 fund to be divided equally each year between two St. Paul area high school students, a boy and a girl. It was to be given to students who demonstrated "excellence in the classroom, in varsity competition, and in the community."

Dave Winfield announced the scholarship at a press conference in the Martin Luther King, Jr., Recreational Center in his own home town, St. Paul.

"The award itself," he said at the conference, "is not the important thing. What is more important is that when individuals try to attain these awards, they better themselves and make the community a better place to live in."

The names of the winners of the scholarship were to be inscribed on a huge plaque to be installed at the King Center recreational facilities; the winners would also receive a miniature duplicate of the plaque.

Dave was understandably quite excited about everything involved in the scholarship fund he had started. First, it carried his name. Or, first perhaps, because he was giving back to his people and his community something they had given him.

"Wait till you see the plaque," he said, so obviously pleased. "It's going to be a beauty to end all plaques. I am very proud and honored to have all this done in my name."

Then Dave recalled his own education. He had recognized early that he must prepare himself for a profession other than sports because a sports career might be severely limited. So he added, "I would like to emphasize that the winners will be primarily good students and potential leading citizens of the future. They don't have to be great athletes."

Dave could not and would not forget that his brother Steve had been a potentially great athlete who had given that up for work in the communities with underprivileged children. Nor did he forget his responsibilities to the people and community from which he came; and he remembered how much the white coach at his neighborhood playground had been his mentor, advisor, even foster father.

"I would like young people to model their lives after me," he said.

He wasn't setting himself up as a paragon of virtue or a symbol of success; he was thinking of himself as someone who had beaten the syndromes of the ghetto and achieved the success and respect he wished for every kid who was burdened with an underprivileged environment.

"The greatest gift I can give," he said, "is if this scholarship becomes a vehicle for others to reach their ideals."

There was an ambivalence about Dave Winfield that is not uncommon. There was the honest-to-goodness pride in his own accomplishments, which were not small by any measure; he also felt something of a fear of that pride: "Pride goeth before a fall." He knew that well enough. He knew, too, that an accident of fate might strip him suddenly and completely of all that he had accomplished. Dave Winfield was, is, a thinking man. And he knew deep down that pride does not make a man, or a life; it is the deed, the accomplishment, that fashions the man and his life.

It's difficult to think of Dave Winfield as humble. It is easy to interpret his speeches to the press as self-serving, self-idolizing, even arrogant.

But Dave Winfield is possessed of a very earnest humility, something he got from his mother, Arline. And if his speech is sometimes abrasive and if sometimes he sounds like a man blowing his own horn, it is only Dave Winfield telling you exactly what he thinks and believes.

"I always considered myself a quiet leader," he says, and, whether you think differently or not, that is what he believes, and you can take it or leave it.

There was one difference. When it came to baseball contracts, and the negotiations for baseball contracts, Dave did little or no talking. His good friend Al Frohman would take care of all that.

8

"Dohvid" Is
an All-Star

Long before Al Frohman handled the negotiations between Dave Winfield and George Steinbrenner, he had been instrumental in raising the
Winfield standard of living. At first his "advice" to Winfield had been
more or less casual, not the agent-client representation that was to come
later. In 1975 Winfield's salary climbed to about $40,000, and that was
due to Frohman's sagacity. A year later the annual stipend was $57,000, a
healthy hike for a .267 hitter. Frohman really didn't get into tough
negotiations until after 1976, when Winfield batted .283. Now Frohman
had the ammunition with which to open fire on the Padres.

Al Frohman's father was a Brooklyn rabbi, musician, and kosher
caterer. The elder Frohman, although an astute businessman, was also
kind and generous, according to a story Al Frohman gave a reporter.
Many years ago Rabbi Frohman saw a young man named Victor Cruz
scavenging in a garbage can in the Brownsville section of Brooklyn. He
took the hungry Puerto Rican home for dinner and Cruz stayed on with
the family for twenty-three years. Frohman also befriended a black man
named Al Washington, who became a kind of family retainer, and he too
stayed with the Frohmans. When the patriarch Frohman died in 1953,

Cruz vanished temporarily and was subsequently discovered at the grave. Cruz seemed unable to exist without the rabbi who had so lovingly befriended him and he died a few months later. When Mrs. Frohman passed away some ten years afterwards, she left part of the estate to Washington.

Al Frohman was originally destined for a career in music. At least he started out that way, attending the prestigious Juilliard School of Music, but when he was mustered out of the army, his father had other ideas for Al's future. He said, "Music isn't for you. There's not enough money there. You go into business with me." Al Frohman did, and he prospered.

Back in the 1930s Rabbi Frohman had been chaplain to the old Brooklyn Dodgers, which partly explains Al's interest in baseball. He began dabbling in the agentry business with "advice" to Cleon Jones of the Mets, and then later imparted his wisdom to Joe Ferguson of the Dodgers and Jerry Turner of the San Diego Padres.

It was in 1974 that Jerry Koosman suggested to Dave that he ought to call on Frohman, that Frohman might be able to get Dave what he wanted from the Padres. Frohman had moved to Los Angeles, and purchased a home in Encino. He is wealthy, independent, but you wouldn't know it by looking at him. He is short and paunchy. At 46 back in 1974, he looked 56. He walks, or rather shuffles, like an old man, or slumps like an old man in his chair. He sighs a lot, blinks his eyes a lot, and his voice sounds tired. But as Dave Winfield, the Padres, and everyone else in baseball would learn, he knows how to wheel and deal. Dave Winfield couldn't have found a better man to have at his side, both as a friend and as a business agent.

Frohman wasn't particularly impressed by the six-foot-six, 220-pound young fellow who came to see him in his wife's clothing store, where he was helping out for the day back in 1974.

"My wife and I had been around guys like Willie Mays, Cleon Jones, and Jerry Koosman," he explains. "Stars were nothing new to us."

Dave spoke briefly to Al's wife Barbara, then had lunch with Al.

"We talked baseball," says Frohman. "Maybe he asked me something about salaries, but I can't remember," continues Al. "But on the way out, this big kid stops and kisses Barbara on her cheek. I'd never seen anything like that before. That kiss started something that will not end until I die."

That something was an enduring friendship, a friendship that gave both men, as Al Frohman puts it, something they could have found nowhere else.

"I know him better than my father," Dave Winfield says of Al Frohman, "and he knows me better than my father."

Frohman lost 70 pounds and he attributes that loss to Winfield's influence. He couldn't walk ten steps without taking a nitroglycerine tablet for his heart, before he met Dave Winfield. He was taking 150 pills a week; now a bottle of those pills lasts six months; he attributes that to Winfield, too.

"I used to think that anyone and everyone was ready to rob you and cheat you for a quarter. I don't feel that way anymore. I don't lie any more. I feel good about myself. I've learned humility. I've learned you get more with honey than with vinegar."

And he attributes all this to his friendship with David Winfield.

What kind of man is this Winfield that he can bring about such profound changes in another man's way of living, his philosophy, his outlook on life, his character? Jim Williams, who coached Dave in basketball at Minnesota in 1971 and 1972, said he was a very sound, steady, and most reliable young man, who attended his classes regularly, studied hard, worked hard on the basketball court and the baseball diamond, and was liked by everyone. "He wanted to be somebody."

"He was always impressed by successful people," said coach Williams. "He saw these people as models and worked hard to emulate them."

This last is something of a clue as to what David Winfield had in mind for himself. It also pictures David Winfield as a man who consciously works on an image he has carefully thought through. He wasn't going to allow life to shape his character; he was going to build a character that would shape his life.

His teammates at San Diego accused him of having a big ego. It's easy to confuse ego with an objective view of one's self, and of one's value. Dave Winfield was probably one of the few men playing for the Padres who felt his ego was taking a beating, losing ball games day in and day out with a cellar club in San Diego.

Of course Dave Winfield has an ego. He wouldn't be where he is, if he didn't.

"His ego, his position among people is very important to him," says Al Frohman. "If Dave can't get respect and affection, he wants money."

Respect comes first. Maybe that's why when he speaks, his voice is well modulated and his vocabulary rich with polysyllabic words, giving the effect of an affable, well-schooled man, intelligent and direct. Yet, listen carefully to Dave Winfield and you'll recognize that he isn't giving you the whole story, that he's always holding something back, that he's something of a private person, unwilling to reveal himself completely.

He dresses carefully. His manners are impeccable. He is gracious, as when he kissed the cheek of Al's wife, Barbara. He is soft spoken. He is, all 6 feet 6 inches and 220 pounds of him, the gentleman he has molded of himself, and the gentleman he wants others to see, and notice, and respect.

What about the core of David Winfield? What lies under all the spit and polish of the man?

"Dave is soft—like butter," says Al Frohman. "But so is his mother. She's soft and intelligent. That's where he came from."

Almost from the outset the chemistry between Al and Dave worked, blending them into what both insisted was a father-son relationship. They were indeed an odd couple, Winfield at 6 feet 6 inches towering over the 5-foot 8-inch Frohman. Winfield was called "Dohvid" by his mentor, the Jewish version of his first name. Frohman maintained that he wasn't helping Dave for the money involved, only to protect him. There were, of course, any number of people who took that statement with several grains of salt.

If there was some lack of modesty in Winfield's words, there was also a lot of truth. In part it was the realization that he was only one of many blacks who had struggled out of the ghettos through excellence in sports, part of a brotherhood whose physical attributes translated into money. If he sounded arrogant, self-serving, sometimes abrasive, it was also his blunt, articulate honesty showing itself. Winfield has always been a proud man with a disarming smile and an easy, diffident charm that tends to mute the horn he blows for himself.

However, when it came to negotiating a new contract with the Padres for 1977, Winfield stepped away and let Al Frohman handle everything. Frohman did all the talking, all the way through spring training and into July.

Yet, according to Buzzie Bavasi, president of the Padres, he and Winfield had come to an agreement as early as January. That was what he told the press.

"All I know," Bavasi said, "is that when I finished talking with Dave, I patted him on the back and said, 'I'm glad we reached an agreement. I don't mind spending money when it's for a good cause, so go out and have yourself a helluva year.'

"Then he told me, 'Buzzie, I feel good and I'm going to go out this year and be the superstar everybody thinks I can be.' That was it."

But Winfield signed no papers, and according to Frohman, it wasn't the money, but the insurance that went with it.

"Would you drive a car without having insurance?" Frohman asked rhetorically, then answered his own question, "Of course not. If Dave signs a three-year contract and gets injured in the first year of it and can't play, we want to be sure he still gets paid his full contract."

Buzzi Bavasi countered, "They want guaranteed payments no matter what happens. Well, suppose Dave goes out and gets himself injured riding a motorcycle? Should we be responsible if he gets hurt off the playing field and can't fulfill his part of it? If he is injured playing baseball, then the contract takes care of that."

While the controversy continued, Kroc made some moves intended to strengthen the team. There were some new faces replacing old faces in the springtime of the year. Gone were veterans Willie McCovey, Willie Davis, and Tito Fuentes. Kroc had shelled out some money, getting former World Series hero Gene Tenace and relief pitcher Rollie Fingers from the Oakland Athletics. Slugger George Hendrick was obtained from Cleveland. On paper, the 1977 Padres looked much improved, especially at the plate. Winfield, it appeared, was not the only hitter in the lineup who warranted respect.

The Padres continued to be losers. It was almost as if it were foreordained, as if it came with the territory. But Dave Winfield reaped his share of headlines in defeat or victory. When they lost, the local headlines read:

WINFIELD BAT BOOMS AMID PITCHING WOES.
PADRES FAIL TO CASH IN ON WINFIELD'S TORRID HITTING PACE.

When San Diego managed to win a game, the headlines reflected Winfield's part in it:

PADRES TAKE TWO ON WINFIELD BAT.
UNSIGNED WINFIELD SHINES FOR PADRES.

By the end of the first week in May Winfield was leading the club in hits with 36, in runs batted in with 24, in stolen bases with 5. He was batting a steady .319, and tied with Doug Rader in home runs. Yet he expressed little satisfaction with his individual performance.

"I hate it because we're losing," he said. "But I can't let it get me down."

The Padres weren't too thrilled with their record either. Taking stock of the situation, the San Diego brass realized they had to strengthen the pitching staff with a front-line starter. The logical move called for them to swap one unhappy outfielder for one proven pitcher. Winfield was playing without a contract, at 80 percent of his 1976 salary. If, at the end of the season he was not signed, he would become a free agent and the Padres would get nothing in exchange. Jon Matlack of the Mets, a dandy southpaw with a winning record, was available, but the New York Mets would not let him go cheaply. A hitter like Winfield might pry him loose. Both the Padres and Mets had a series of preliminary talks, just on a skirmishing basis.

A Matlack-for-Winfield trade was not the kind of deal that could be kept secret. These were a pair of front line stars, starters on any team in either league. Matlack knew about the possibility and he had no objections. Winfield, on the other hand, was not anxious to uproot and go to another city, at least not yet. When the news reached him, Winfield responded in a very effective manner.

Playing against those same Mets, Winfield unloosed a barrage of hits that knocked off New York in both ends of a twin bill. In the first game he belted a homer and two singles to drive in three runs. In the second game he batted home the winning run.

No trade.

By May 20th Dave was hitting .327 and playing without a contract. By June 1st he had upped his home-run total to 10, his runs batted in to 42. He was tied with Dave Parker of the Pittsburgh Pirates and Rod Carew of Minnesota for the most hits in the majors with 66. Still no contract.

When the press put it to him about the stalled contract, Winfield, perhaps understandably testy, replied, "I refuse to do my negotiating through the media. I expect to be treated fairly, but I feel strongly about my security."

When pressed about a possible trade, he responded, "Hey, I like this city. I like the people here. We used to draw 5,000 to 6,000 a game. Now we draw a million and a half a season. I like to think I'm part of the reason for that."

To reinforce his position, Winfield stressed the undeniable fact that he didn't have to remain in San Diego after 1977 unless he felt strongly about the city. He said, "If I wasn't happy and didn't want to play here, we wouldn't even have bothered to negotiate with the Padres. I would just play out my option and that would be it."

The San Diego press played up the disagreement between Winfield-Frohman and the Padres front office, since there was practically nothing to say about the team's performance. John McNamara had been dismissed early in the season, replaced by Alvin Dark, who had been an outstanding shortstop with the New York Giants during his playing career, and then managed the Giants when they won the 1962 National League pennant. Dark couldn't turn the team around either. The blame could be placed squarely on the pitching staff. Over the first 81 games, a full half-season, only one pitcher had managed a complete game.

The Padres were in an untenable position. The sole shaft of sunlight seeping through the clouds of defeat was Dave Winfield, and the team seemed hell bent on losing him, regardless of the cost in fans' good will. Indeed, some wits in the stands had put a banner on display which read: "Keep Dave, Trade Buzzie."

It was no secret that Bavasi and Frohman were not overly fond of each other. Frohman was accused of preventing Winfield from signing a contract which the big outfielder had evidently agreed to, according to Bavasi. To a certain extent, Frohman admitted, Bavasi was telling the truth; but the deal fell apart.

"We did shake hands and agree on financial figures," Frohman said.

"But a contract is not formulated just on monies. I told Mike Port [a Padres executive] the contract did not read the way we asked. He said it would be changed in the agreement. It was not changed in the agreement."

At the same time Frohman also confessed that the original asking price had gone up. "We took a gamble by not signing," he explained. "Now Dave has proved himself. We think he's worth what some other guys are getting."

Frohman had a point there. By July 4th Winfield was batting .298 with 17 home runs and 60 runs batted in. If he felt any pressure, his stats certainly didn't indicate any. Yet Frohman insisted that his client was growing more unhappy daily.

"I hate to see Dave aggravated like this over a matter of pennies," Frohman said. "I thought we had a deal yesterday. We were that close. I thought it was going to be inked. Then Bavasi didn't show up today and I don't know what to think."

Actually, Bavasi wasn't there because he was at home, ill. He said that Frohman and Winfield had changed their minds for the fourth time. Told that Frohman claimed it "was just a matter of pennies," Bavasi took issue.

"Is $200,000 pennies?" Bavasi asked, then added, "It's pennies when it's somebody else's money."

Oddly, the boss himself, Ray Kroc, did not enter the negotiations, despite the fact that it was his money being bandied about in such a cavalier fashion. He had paid out millions getting Tenace and Fingers in the free agent draft and they weren't helping the team out of the doldrums, so nobody could blame him if he had become sick and tired of the whole situation.

By July 4th the situation had been milked dry of its news value. That was the date on which Winfield-Frohman and the Padres came to terms. The full details of most contracts are seldom made public, because these legal documents with their multiple clauses and reams of fine print could only confuse the average fan. Most educated guesses placed the dollar value at $1.3 million over a four-year period, and that was probably accurate enough for most purposes.

The fans seemed satisfied too. When Winfield was introduced in the ball park the night following his signing, he was given a roaring ovation which did not subside until he emerged from the dugout smiling broadly and waving his cap. For Winfield, who always thrived on public approval, it was a kind of vindication.

"It's a big relief to get this thing behind me," he said, referring to the contract. "There has been a tremendous amount of pressure on me. When people thought I might be playing out my option, that's all they wanted to talk about. I became a point of controversy and I never wanted that. I'm a baseball player, not a politician. Now, at last, we can talk about baseball again."

And baseball talk was on every San Diego fan's lips some two weeks later, this time about Dave Winfield's performance in the All-Star game at Yankee Stadium. Winfield was not selected on the ballot but rather as one of the reserves, meaning he would not start. He didn't seem to mind.

"I've waited a long time for this, four years in the major leagues. I'm twenty-five and I'm ready. I have arrived," the grinning outfielder commented.

Winfield was ensconced in the dugout as the National League teed off on Baltimore's Jim Palmer in the first inning. Joe Morgan opened the game with a blast into the right field seats, then Dave Parker singled, George Foster doubled for another run, and Greg Luzinski hit one out to make the score 4-0.

Palmer survived the second inning, but when Steve Garvey opened the third with a blast into the left-center field bullpen, American League manager Billy Martin strolled out to give Palmer the hook.

"What took you so long?" asked Palmer.

Winfield's first trip to the plate came in the sixth inning. Lefthander Dave LaRoche delivered one over the outside corner and Dave lined a shot into right field. Jim Rice got his glove on the ball but his hand hit the wall and it dropped to the turf. Winfield was credited with a double.

"I hit it hard enough but not high enough," was Winfield's evaluation of his clout.

In the eighth Winfield pulled a single to left, scoring two runs. Since the American League rallied to come within two runs, Winfield's RBIs were the game-winners.

Undoubtedly Winfield was elated by his play, but surely there must have been some spice added by the column written by *Minneapolis Star* sportswriter Max Nichols, the same scribe who had cast doubts over Winfield's career with his article decrying Winfield's lack of team spirit.

Nichols wrote, "For Dave Winfield, who grew up on the playgrounds of St. Paul, last night's two hits in two at-bats signaled the start of a new era for him as a star athlete . . . to Winfield it was a coming-out party that was to be expected, a graduation to stardom, a confirmation of destiny, not fantasy. . . ."

For Dave Winfield, the 1977 season was his finest to date. He was the Padres top offensive performer, leading the club in practically every department, including runs (104), hits (169), doubles (29), home runs (25) and runs batted in (92). He had two good hitting streaks, one from May 3rd to the 21st in which he hit safely in 16 straight games, and another from June 14th to the 27th for 13 consecutive games.

But those were first-half statistics, the good part. At the end of 81 games he was hitting .298 with 17 homers and 60 RBIs. But down the stretch section of the season he batted .249 with eight added homers and 32 additional runs batted in. His final average was .275.

It was a duplication of his 1976 season in many respects, and various theories were advanced for his second-half slumps. According to one source, once he had the security of a long term contract, he had nothing to prove to the front office and could rest on his first-half laurels.

Winfield dismissed that brainstorm out of hand. "The contract had nothing to do with what happened," he said. "I have too much pride not to play my best, regardless of the money."

Well then, was Winfield taking good care of himself physically? "Of course," was the answer. "I get my rest. I have some business interests outside of baseball, but I back off if I feel they're beginning to interfere with the way I play."

True, Winfield longed to play with a winning team, and losing seemed to be a way of life with the Padres, but apparently he had put down roots in San Diego. He owned a condominium there, he made television commercials free of charge for the Urban League, and he spent thousands of dollars to provide tickets for kids who couldn't afford to go to games. "Winfield Pavillion" was a section in the bleachers where underprivileged youngsters by the hundreds would be given free tickets, courtesy of Dave Winfield. Winfield even arranged free soda pop, sandwiches, and other concession items.

The Padres, meanwhile, were also mindful of Winfield's second-half declines. Ray Kroc had doled out several million dollars for players and only once had his team finished as high as fourth place. He was disenchanted with his manager, with his front office, with baseball itself, and his mutterings were not pleasant. Who could blame him? Wasn't there *anybody* he could call in to deliver a winner?

He hadn't been able to buy respectability for his club despite the acquisition of big names such as Rollie Fingers and Gene Tenace. Since money wasn't the answer, perhaps a trade was. There were holes to be plugged, at third base and on the mound. But, as the old adage had it, you've got to give something of value to get something of value.

Kroc had very little of value on the San Diego roster, but there was one highly marketable player whom he knew a number of teams were interested in. That was his twenty-six-year-old right fielder, Dave Winfield.

Dave Winfield in his Yankee uniform.

Dave Winfield, Central High's outstanding pitcher, hurled a no-hit game in the Minnesota State High School Tournament at St. Paul on June 3, 1969.

Winfield displays his college pitching form. In his senior year at the University of Minnesota his record was 13-2, an astounding performance for a man who would become a multimillionaire slugger and outfielder. Even then he was wearing pinstripes.

Winfield of the University of Minnesota Golden Gophers. His *forte* was the big leap for the rebound.

An all-around athlete, Winfield was drafted by professional baseball, basketball, and football teams, the last despite the fact that he didn't even play college football.

Winfield stretches his 6 foot 6 inch frame before stepping to the plate for the San Diego Padres.

The Winfield follow-through. At the beginning of his career Dave had a hitch in his swing, but he overcame it.

Winfield edges off second base. He's considered one of the best base runners in the majors.

Determination on his face, Dave shows his base-running style.

Winfield moving toward second base as Met infielder awaits the throw.

It's a close play as Dave slides hard into third base.

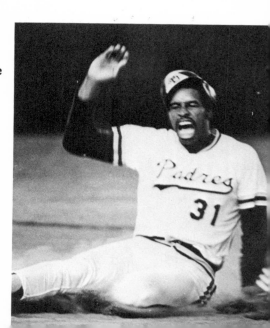

Teammate Bobby Tolan gives Dave the grip as Winfield crosses the plate after hitting a home run.

Dave starts his batting swing.

Winfield standing beside Mike Schmidt of the Phillies at the 1980 All-Star Game.

"It's part of being a Yankee," said Dave as he took a subway ride in New York City during his first few days in town in November 1980, just after signing his $23 million contract.

Dave with Yankee owner George Steinbrenner.

Dave tries on his new Yankee cap. Reggie Jackson, who would be Dave's teammate for one year before signing with the Angels, looks on.

Dave adjusts to his new surroundings in the Yankee locker room.

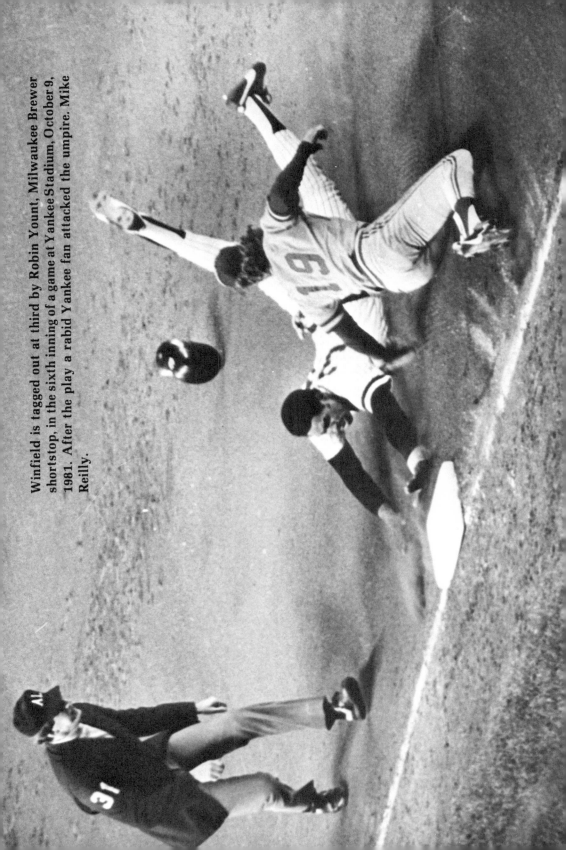

Winfield is tagged out at third by Robin Yount, Milwaukee Brewer shortstop, in the sixth inning of a game at Yankee Stadium, October 9, 1981. After the play a rabid Yankee fan attacked the umpire. Mike Reilly.

At Manhattan's famed Studio 54, Dave dances with actress Danielle Dourneaux during a benefit for the Muscular Dystrophy Association.

9

Captain of
the Padres

The year 1978 opened quite pleasantly for Dave Winfield. On January 31st, the California South District of Optimist International awarded its Friend of Youth Service Award to the San Diego right fielder.

"David Winfield's ability as a professional baseball player is well known throughout the baseball world," began the citation. "However, his contribution to youths perhaps is not widely known. It is for this reason that California South District enthusiastically recommended him for the Optimist International Friend of Youth Service Award."

It was a nice, warm gesture and Winfield was not just a little pleased. However, the baseball part of his life was not quite so smooth. The winter meetings resounded with echoes of trades in the making, trades the Padres sought to engineer, using Mike Ivie and Dave Winfield as bait. Somewhere along the line Al Frohman got into the picture as Ivie's agent, but only peripherally.

Winfield had attended the winter meeting in Hawaii, and while he was flattered by all the attention he received, by the time the gathering broke up he was somewhat confused.

"I never expected to put on a Padres uniform again," Dave said later. "It seemed the other teams didn't want anybody but me."

One of the proposed trades required the services of a computer expert to explain all its parts. It was a four-way swap which included the Philadelphia Phillies, the Cleveland Indians, the New York Yankees, and the San Diego Padres, and only the good Lord knew who might have gotten the best of it.

Initially, Philadelphia would deal catcher Bob Boone and perhaps outfielder Jay Johnstone to Cleveland for pitcher Dennis Eckersley. Cleveland would trade catcher Boone and third baseman Buddy Bell to the Yankees for catcher Thurman Munson and another outfielder. The Yankees, with two third basemen on their hands, would swap their incumbent, Graig Nettles, plus pitcher Ed Figueroa, for Dave Winfield.

Interestingly, it was reported that Yankee owner George Steinbrenner turned down the deal.

Another tentative deal had Winfield going to the Dodgers. San Diego wanted pitcher Rick Rhoden and catcher Steve Yaeger. Los Angeles countered with Rhoden, outfielder Lee Lacey, and a couple of rookies.

No deal.

The Mike Ivie exchange had its beginnings the previous season. Manager Alvin Dark had asked Ivie to switch over to third base, but Ivie insisted on playing first base, his normal position. Ivie's refusal cost him a brief suspension and loss of some salary. That was one of the reasons John McNamara had been fired. Dark convinced the front office that Ivie would play third under his direction, whereupon the Padres sold Doug Rader. But Ivie wasn't happy and made no bones about it, so that the Padres had to recall Tucker Ashford from their Hawaii farm team. Ashford couldn't handle the job, batting .217 and struggling at third base.

At the winter meetings, Ray Kroc was willing to part with Ivie for "yesterday's loaf of bread." He was subsequently dealt to San Francisco for Derrel Thomas, but not before Al Frohman had made his pitch in behalf of Ivie.

Frohman hinted that Ivie might be amenable to trying third base if he could renegotiate his contract, which called for $60,000 in 1977, $85,000 in 1978, and $110,000 in 1979.

"It would be like tearing a dollar bill in half," suggested Frohman in his usual mild manner. "Give him half, and tell him he gets the other half at the end of the season when he's shown he can produce. Give him some incentive, tell him he's your third baseman, and I think he would go to spring training and respond to the challenge."

The Ivie-Thomas trade made Frohman's pitch purely academic, but the attempted renegotiation demonstrated the agent's ability to turn a phrase.

Still another big change was in the offing. Before the season got under way, Alvin Dark was fired as manager, replaced by pitching coach Roger Craig. The switch drew the approval of many of the players.

Both as a manager and player, Alvin Dark had proved he belonged in the big leagues. He had been the National League Rookie of the Year in 1948 as a member of the pennant-winning Boston Braves; then, traded to the New York Giants, he helped them win the flag in 1951 and 1954. In 1962 he had managed the San Francisco Giants to a pennant, then took the Oakland Athletics to the top in 1974 and 1975. He had been managing for eleven years before he came to the Padres. There he lasted less than one season.

Alvin Dark had too many offbeat plays, the players said. He had too many signs. He complicated things when they didn't have to be complicated. Also, Dark didn't know how to approach his players on a personal level; he seemed distant, in sharp contrast to the caring attitude of John McNamara.

Roger Craig was cut from a different pattern. He had been around the majors as a pitcher for some years, tasting both success and failure. The lowest point in his active career came with the expansion New York Mets, when he lost so consistently, despite some creditable performances, that he became a pitiable figure. Becoming the Padres third manager in eleven months shouldered him with an unenviable burden.

One of Craig's first moves was to hire Billy Herman as his batting coach. Previously, Alvin Dark had been his own batting coach in his spare time, and he was a good one too, except that the job really called for a full-time coach. Herman, who had been elected to the Hall of Fame in 1975, had been one of the premier second basemen in all of baseball. He had played in every All-Star game from 1934 through 1943, as regularly as the game itself, and had been on pennant winners as a member of the Chicago Cubs and Brooklyn Dodgers.

There had been additional housecleaning previously. Both Buzzie Bavasi and his son, Peter, were gone. Bob Fontaine had been moved into the general manager's slot.

When Craig was handed the reins on March 21st, he had only 17 spring training games left to prepare himself for opening day. He had an infield that wasn't set, a mixed bag of pitchers, and an outfield with good power. His trio of Oscar Gamble, George Hendrick, and Dave Winfield had clouted a total of 79 home runs the previous year (Gamble had 31 for the White Sox). His catcher was Gene Tenace, but the veteran had not been a ball of fire at the plate.

It was then that Winfield, the "veteran" of four and a half years with the Padres, asked permission to call a team meeting. He had, in a way, assumed the mantle of team leadership without having the honor officially bestowed upon him.

"In the past, we haven't had common goals," he said when the players had gathered. "I'm talking about the players, the manager, the coaches, middle management, and the owner. Now I see a change.

"It's time we merged our talents into a team. We've got ballplayers who gave 100 percent of their ability and others who gave something less. We can't depend on one or two people to do the job every day. If they fail somebody has to take over.

"We've reached the point where we must assert ourselves. Last week we played an exhibition game against the Minnesota Twins, a bunch of no-names, and they gave us a good whipping. The Twins deserve credit. They really cared about winning.

"That has to be our direction. We've got to become aggressive, a team that forces errors, and wins on the other fellows' mistakes. We've been the patsy too long."

It was a stirring speech and Craig was evidently impressed by it. Just prior to the opening game against San Francisco Craig made an announcement:

"I'm appointing Dave Winfield captain of the Padres."

"I was somewhat surprised," was Winfield's reaction, "but I'm very happy about it."

Then the new captain of the San Diego Padres, their first in the team's history, led the team to a come-from-behind victory over the Giants, putting them at the head of the National League West, for one day anyway.

The Giants led, 2-0, into the seventh inning when Oscar Gamble drove in a run with a sacrifice fly. An inning later Winfield found the range with a tremendous drive into the stands for a home run.

"It was kind of up to me in the eighth," he said later, "to see if I could ignite something. The homer did it."

Following the homer, George Hendrick singled, then three walks forced in the winning run.

After the game Roger Craig said, "I might be smarter than I think I am, waiting until today to name Dave our captain. This naming of a captain was not a decision I made on the spur of the moment. Dave played like this was the seventh game of the World Series. He really had himself a day."

Willie McCovey, playing first base for the Giants again after his tenure with the Padres, said of Winfield, "Making him captain will really do a lot for him. That may be the little extra incentive he needs to keep going all out when he otherwise might not. Dave Winfield is the type who can carry a whole team. I've seen him do it."

Winfield and his bat were out of the starting blocks with a rain of base hits. On that opening day he had a single, a double, and a home run. Two days later he tripled home three runs, the next night he drove in four runs with a single and a homer, and after that he rapped two singles, stole a base, and scored the winning run in a 3-2 victory over the Atlanta Braves.

"I took it easy all winter," he said. "I took it easy in spring training. But I was ready when the bell rang."

Of the first 18 runs the Padres scored in 1978, Winfield drove in 8. In the first 23 games he batted better than .300, banged six homers and drove in 18 runs. With such heroics the Padres should have been right up there fighting for the lead, but such was not the case.

The pitching was, to be kind about it, less than adequate. In the first five games the Padres averaged 3.6 runs but still lost three of the five. In a later game against Atlanta, the Padres were leading, 5-0, going into the bottom of the third. Atlanta ganged up on starter Dave Freisleben and he was out of there after four and a third innings, having given up eight hits, three walks, and three runs. The Padres carried a 7-5 lead into the ninth. With two out, a single, and back-to-back home runs, Atlanta beat them, 8-7.

"Dave is carrying most of the offensive load," Craig said ruefully, "but we aren't getting good pitching."

The explosive situation came to a head in mid-June with the Padres at 24-32, eight games below the .500 mark. The team was in town for a 19-game home stand, and pitcher Randy Jones, the San Diego player representative, remarked that the club had about ten players with a pretty shitty attitude.

"They don't give a good goddamn," he said. "It's beyond control."

Jones had made that statement for the record, and manager Craig held a 35-minute meeting behind closed doors. Evidently Winfield's brave words at the beginning of the season had little effect because the team's record indicated as much, and there were some known malcontents on the roster.

After listening to several players speak their minds, Craig told the press, "It was the best meeting I've ever attended. We decided there wasn't enough togetherness on the team, that we need to pull together, pull harder for each other."

It was an eminently forgettable series of cliches that the manager uttered, quite similar in tone and content to captain Winfield's earlier inspirational sermon. Owner Ray Kroc, on the other hand, was in no mood to mince words. He minced, instead, the hides of his paid employees.

Anyone who has ever thought that George Steinbrenner of the Yankees knows how to flay a baseball team is sadly mistaken. Mr. Steinbrenner is a rank amateur when it comes to chastising the hired help, as compared with the owner of the San Diego Padres. He was absolutely awesome, and his tirade must rank among the greatest outbursts of frustration in the history of professional sports.

"I'm sick and tired of the way this ball club has been playing," he began. "It's pitiful. I'm thoroughly disgusted."

Recall that on opening day in 1974 Mr. Kroc had made a few

well-chosen remarks over the public address system, crediting his hire-
lings with "some of the most stupid ball playing I've ever seen." That
was mild. Now Kroc really laid it on the line.

"Gene Tenace needs to go to an eye doctor," Kroc went on. "He can't
tell a strike from a ball. He hasn't given the club one thing since we got
him. He kept saying if he played every day he'd improve. Well, he's been
in there every day and he hasn't done a damn thing. All he wants to do is
walk. Well, we can't win games waiting for walks.

"I'm telling you, Tenace is the most overrated ballplayer on this club.
He's a disgrace. He's being paid to hit and he can't hit. Nobody in either
league wants him and we're paying him a premium price [$1.8 million
over six years].

"Randy Jones says there are ten guys on this team who don't want to
win. No one said who they are, but we have some pretty good ideas. I'll
tell you one thing, if they keep on this way, they'll be in the minors.

"I can't understand it. These dumb sons of bitches didn't want to play
for Alvin Dark. Now do they want to play for Roger Craig? Not a damn
bit. And I'm not criticizing Roger. He's done a great job with the
material he's got.

"I'm thoroughly disgusted with professional athletes in general. I just
don't understand. Don't these guys aspire to some success? Don't they
have some drive, some spirit?

"Buzzie Bavasi had a lot of these guys on the team when I came here. I
told him to get rid of them, that they can't win. Well, I look around and
some of them are still here.

"The Yankees get rid of guys like that. The Dodgers get rid of them,
Cincinnati gets rid of them. You have to. They can't win for you."

Quite a tirade and not without some sense, but Ray Kroc was just
warming up.

"I don't think they've got any guts or pride. They may not give a damn,
but I've got news for them. I do."

He was steaming, and steaming right along.

"I want ballplayers. I'm not going to subsidize idiots. Whoever heard
of a bastard who can't hit being paid a major league salary? I don't know
what these guys want. You give them a private plane, a players' lounge,
everything under the sun, and they still respond like juveniles. Only four

players on this team are responding: Ozzie Smith, Derrel Thomas, Randy Jones, and Gaylord Perry. The rest are demanding major league salaries and playing like high school kids."

Tenace wasn't terribly disturbed by Kroc's outburst. After all, he had played for the button-busting Charley Finley.

"I'm just glad it was me he attacked," said the veteran, who was hitting at .227, with six homers and 20 runs batted in for the first 60 games of the season, "instead of one of our younger players. I really wish he hadn't said those things but I can understand his frustration. He wants a championship club and he's frustrated. But all I can do is keep going out there and bust my butt giving 100 percent."

Why wasn't Winfield mentioned while Kroc was sounding off? Was he lost in the shuffle? Or, was it that Winfield was indeed pulling his weight, earning his keep, and therefore was above the hassle? Obviously, it was the latter. By the end of June he had 14 home runs and was tied with Cincinnati's George Foster for the RBI lead with 54.

Craig, however, had to make some kind of move in order to show Kroc that he was trying. He announced, with the approval of the front office, that he intended to platoon Oscar Gamble and George Hendrick in right field.

Upon hearing this tidbit, Winfield said, "I think I'm the best right fielder in baseball."

Craig must have concurred. He dropped the proposal and Dave stayed put in right field.

Whether it was Ray Kroc or a case of the guilty conscience needing no accuser, the Padres caught fire and began to move up. Winfield was in good part responsible. Over the month of June he batted .333, averaging better than one RBI per game, a total of 31 runs batted in over 29 games. Dave and Vida Blue ended in a tie for Player of the Month.

On July 4th the Padres suddenly found themselves playing one game over .500 ball. It was a 7-5 win over the Giants that propelled them into such a relatively exalted position. How did they win that game? In the very first inning Winfield clubbed one into the seats for the third grand slam of his career. If one cared to study team statistics, it was the team's fourth victory in a row, their 12th in the last 16 games and their 17th in their last 25.

But Winfield wasn't happy. He had been forced to play some games

both leagues. As for Perry, he was headed for a 20-wins-plus season.

As the Padres and Winfield rolled on, the Winfield-Frohman dynamic duo came up with a new business venture which received ample coverage in the press. It took the form of a kind of recreational development—"an optimal family health resort"—which, supposedly, would attract a number of professional athletes who might live there and also act as "celebrity counselors." Named "Superstar Village," the land site consisted of 46 acres on Mission Bay, just alongside Interstate-5 Road.

As it turned out, the project never got off the ground. When the city fathers were approached, all they were shown were some drawings and outlines projecting the number of units to be built. There were no financial statements, merely much enthusiasm.

Doug Best, the former mayor of Escondido, California, was also consulted by Frohman and Winfield. The statement he made was later quoted in a national sports magazine:

"They came in all peaches and cream and we cautioned them about the hurdles. . . . My opinion was that Dave Winfield was a very sincere young man who had gotten some very bad advice real estate-wise. What we saw was very premature and very shoddily prepared. If anyone could kill a deal, Frohman could."

During all these preliminary negotiations the names of several notable athletes were mentioned, including those of Steve Garvey, Pete Rose, and Kareem Abdul-Jabbar. Their relationship with the project was unclear, but perhaps by innuendo or rumor, they were supposedly among those backing Superstar Village. All denied any participation in the venture; indeed, they said their names had been mentioned without permission.

In reply, Al Frohman stated, "We never said 'Steve Garvey.' What we actually said was that this was the *kind* of project that would attract the Steve Garveys. There were a lot of athletes interested in this, but we never signed any papers or contracts."

Whatever the outcome of the real estate venture, Winfield kept his mind on baseball, which was, after all, his primary source of income. He kept making contact with his bat and making catches with his glove, giving Ray Kroc no cause to regret the salary he was paying.

Even though the Padres were finally winning more often than they

91

were losing, Winfield wasn't satisfied. In his zeal to go all the way to the top, he made statements more suitable for a general manager than one of the guys on the payroll.

"No matter how close we come to the top," he said in the waning days of 1978, "it still comes down to the fact that we didn't make it. Even though this is going to be our best season, we still could end up in fourth place. Never finishing higher than fourth in ten years, that's a sorry picture.

"We need to make some trades. We need to go after some free agents who can help the club. We need a catcher, a third baseman, a second baseman, and more righthanded pitching. We can't just sit back and hope the rookies are going to fill the voids. We've got to go for more gusto and we've got to go for it now."

The Padres did end up fourth, but a winning fourth, 84-78, only 11 games out of first place. Manager Roger Craig was invited back for 1979. The Padres were a young team—with just a couple of exceptions—and improvement was more than likely.

As for Winfield, he had enjoyed the finest season of his professional career. Far from tapering off, over the final 35 games he batted a torrid .374, and his final average was .308, fifth highest in the National League. Once more he led the Padres in almost every possible offensive category: in hits with 181, in doubles with 30, in homers with 24, in runs batted in with 97 and in game-winning hits with 12. His 21 stolen bases ranked third on the Padres.

"I played well at the start, in the middle and at the finish," Dave said of his year's work. "I could look back and say, 'Hey, I did it.'"

Well, said the baseball world, so Dave Winfield has finally arrived. But, can he do it again?

10

The Winfield
Pavilion

"Life has been good to me," Dave Winfield said as spring training got under way in March of 1979. "I live in a great area, have lots of nice friends. I've been lucky, baseball has been beneficial to my life-style. It's a part of me, like music or other people. I wake up to music, go to sleep to music. I like all kinds. It's the same way with people.

"I've been invited to the White House, I've been the guest of foreign governments, but I never want to get too removed from the common man. One thing anyone needs to know is, you meet the same people going up that you meet coming down."

Winfield was basking in the glow of his accomplishments, a very normal reaction after his superior season the previous year. He had lived up to the predictions that had been made since he joined the Padres almost a half-dozen years earlier. And he had been honored by so many organizations that it was difficult to keep track of them.

He had received citations from the Jewish community, from the Mexican and American Foundation, from the Boys Club of San Diego, from the National Asthma Center, from the American Legion, the

Chamber of Commerce, the National Conference of Christians and Jews. He had, indeed, become a solid citizen of Southern California.

Winfield had adjusted, not only to his urban environment, but also to his talents on the ball field. What had been a hitch in his swing was largely eliminated, although he had and would again fall into bad habits at the plate from time to time. He had, at last, resolved not to try to swing for the seats every time he had a bat in his hands. In effect he had butted heads with the dimensions of the San Diego home park and conceded defeat.

"It took me three years to figure that out," he admitted. "When people around the league see me they figure I should be hitting 40 homers a season. But not in this park."

The stadium measures 330 feet down the foul lines and 420 feet to dead center. A 17-foot wall, the highest in baseball, had to be negotiated before a ball could sail into the stands.

"Guys like Jim Rice, George Foster, Greg Luzinski, they run out of here crying," Winfield observed. "They say they hit the ball hard and it doesn't go anywhere. I figure I'm going to hit 20 or 25 home runs a year and I'm not going to ask myself to hit much more than that."

Winfield also claimed that he had learned patience and where the strike zone was located. "I learned that sometimes it's better to take a walk than make an out on a bad pitch. Now I have more confidence and experience."

These were good words, but not completely accurate. There were times, such as the May 22nd game against the Dodgers when the Padres were down 4-0, when Winfield let frustration overcome wisdom. Winfield had been walked intentionally in the first inning and singled in the fourth, and when he dug in at the plate in the sixth with two on and two out, he should have known that pitcher Doug Rau wouldn't give him anything to hit. Rau threw four pitches outside and Winfield, in his zeal, struck out.

All was well, however, as the Padres pulled the game out, 7-6. Winfield had two singles, a home run and two intentional walks.

"I knew exactly what they were doing," Winfield said, referring to his strikeout. "They were going to pitch around me. I tried to get a hit to bring us back and I looked bad doing it."

94

Commenting on his two-run homer, he added, "You know those RBIs I got tonight? They were my first in two weeks. And I'm hitting .337! That tells me there are a lot of people on this team playing poorly right now."

Playing with a contender had become almost an obsession with Winfield. Early in the year he had told an interviewer, "We were close enough for a shot at the top last year until the final month of the season. Now I can't be content with fifth, fourth, or even third place. Playing .500 ball can no longer be a goal; that's mediocrity. I'm hoping we're going to be a lot stronger than that this year."

Early in a baseball season, with only a few games played, some batting averages tend to rise astronomically. For example, a player with 9 hits in 20 at-bats is hitting .450, while only 7 hits in 20 at-bats comes to .350, a difference of 100 percentage points. Thus it was partly a mirage to look at Winfield's average toward the end of April and find him leading both leagues with a lofty .426. However, his peers in the majors recognized his ability.

"Winfield is playing in obscurity in San Diego," said John Stearns, the New York Mets catcher. "He ranks alongside Jim Rice and Dave Parker as one of the best players in baseball."

Randy Jones, Winfield's teammate, concurred. "On a national scale I guess you could say he's pretty underrated, but he's certainly not unappreciated on our club. We get on him a lot about his ego, but actually he's just very confident. He does a lot of talking, but he backs it up. He's a lot like Reggie Jackson that way."

If, as Stearns implied, Dave Winfield was one of baseball's best-kept secrets, that was not Winfield's fault. There was never a lack of sportswriters with notebooks at the ready, and Winfield was never at a loss for words.

"My statistics don't adequately show what I do for this club on a day-in, day-out basis," he said. "For instance, runners don't score from second very often on us on a base hit to right field. And they don't often go from first to third on me because they know I can throw them out. That doesn't show up in the statistics, does it?"

Once again, that was mostly true because Winfield certainly did hustle—but not always. In a game against the Phillies, catcher Bob

Boone got an ordinary base hit to right and stretched it into a double. Perhaps Winfield "nonchalanted it" because Boone wasn't noted for his speed, and Winfield wasn't expecting him to keep running. It was merely a lapse in judgment. Padres pitcher Gaylord Perry stated publicly that Winfield was not aggressive enough on that play. Winfield was visibly upset over Perry's remark and said so.

"I didn't appreciate having my behind raked over the coals in the paper by him," he retorted. "I make one mistake and it gets blown up.

"What Gaylord forgets though is that he wouldn't have won the Cy Young Award last year if it hadn't been for me. I was personally responsible for eight or nine of those [21] games he won. Only Rollie Fingers [who was the bellweather of the relief corps] was more instrumental than I was for his great year."

Winfield should have been forgiven his occasional lapses. In mid-May he was leading the league in hits with 51, he had seven triples which proved he was running with abandon, yet the Padres were languishing in fifth place. He constituted most of the San Diego offense. Manager Roger Craig (he would be gone by season's end) lauded his star to the skies, and banged the drum loudly for Winfield's selection by ballot to the All-Star squad. In the past Dave's selection had been almost an afterthought.

"That's why I've always been against the fans getting to vote for the All-Star game," Craig said. "I think the teams should be selected by the managers, the players, or the media because they all have a much better idea which players deserve to be on it."

The starting outfield, Craig insisted, should be Winfield, Dave Parker of Pittsburgh, and George Foster of Cincinnati. To be sure they were three dandies, but there was a flaw in Craig's thinking—none of them was a center fielder. Which proved that even experienced baseball men have blind spots. Winfield might have played center temporarily; he had the range, and certainly the arm, but not the experience.

"Winfield has to be one of the two best outfielders in the league," Craig continued. "Parker is the only one close as far as being able to do so many things. Foster will hit more home runs, but he can't play defense or throw with the other two guys."

As if to solidify his position in the minds of National League fans,

Winfield began systematically to take rival pitchers apart. In a game against Montreal, he crashed two home runs and a single; he also threw a man out at third base. At the time he had the best overall record in the major leagues. The Padres won that game, 6-3. In a previous game against the Mets, big Dave belted two triples and a single. The Padres lost that game, 4-3.

For a long time Winfield had practically begged to be switched from fourth to third in the batting order. He was, he said, tired of leading off the second inning with no one on base, and could be infinitely more productive if he were moved up a notch. Near the end of May, Roger Craig finally decided to try the noble experiment. Winfield responded with renewed vigor. A May 30th game against Atlanta proved the wisdom of the move, when Dave drove in five runs with a single and a home run. In the four games following his placement in the number three slot Winfield drove in nine runs; the Padres won all four games and moved to within five and a half games of the lead. In a game against the Cardinals, Winfield smashed a bases-loaded triple and a single. Over a stretch of 13 games Dave amassed 23 hits in 49 trips to the plate for an astonishing .469 average. Included in the barrage were five home runs, 19 runs batted in and 13 runs scored.

Perhaps it had just been an instinctive feeling on Winfield's part, that for him batting third was better than clean-up. As he put it, "There's no way I can explain it, but it's been working. I was scalding the ball when I was hitting fourth and I've been scalding the ball hitting third, too. But for some reason I've been getting up there with men on base a lot more often in the third spot."

Probably the effect on opposing pitchers had been psychological. In the past, they tried very hard to dispose of the first three men in the lineup, and having done that, they could think about Winfield an inning later. But now pitchers knew they had to face him right away. Concentrating on the first two hitters was a bit more difficult, and without total concentration, any pitcher is dead.

But the good pitchers adjust, mechanically and psychologically. The good hitters, conversely, go off on streaks and then cool off inexplicably. That combination worked on Winfield in mid-June. Suddenly he fell into a terrible slump. It made no difference when or where he batted; he couldn't beg, steal, buy, or borrow a base hit. A nine-game stretch followed in which he went 4-for-28 for .143. The Padres scored only 21 runs and lost seven of the nine games. It became painfully obvious that as Dave Winfield went, so went the Padres.

Although embarrassed by the Padres' poor showing and his own shortcomings, Winfield refused to become overly depressed. He couldn't forget what happened on the field but he tried not to dwell on it. As he put it, "I know there are people who think I'm involved in too many outside activities, but if all I thought about was baseball and the Padres, I'd go crazy."

Winfield announced plans to have his "one-day" Winfield Pavilion in Shea Stadium when the Padres played the Mets. Furthermore, there would be another All-Star game party in Seattle for that city's kids on July 17th. He was as good as his word. At the All-Star party a number of stars, including Pete Rose, regaled some 15,000 youngsters. This party cost something in the vicinity of $15,000. Without doubt that was a bargain, and the kids had a marvelous time.

Having cast his bread upon the waters, Winfield soon learned, much to his satisfaction, that his light was *not* being hidden under a bushel basket. Of all the outfielders on the National League All-Star team, David Winfield received the most votes from the fans, 3,040,567 to be exact, a total second only to the 3,165,546 received by Philadelphia third baseman Mike Schmidt. True, about a million came from fans in the San Diego area, but two thirds of the votes came from other fans, indicating that the National League's paying customers knew full well who Dave Winfield was.

"I'm the first San Diego player ever voted in," Winfield noted. "I would have been satisfied just to start, but to finish so high among all those great players is a tremendous thrill. I hope I can contribute to another National League win and continue to play as well as I am now."

Deep down, Winfield must have felt delighted the day he learned about his total vote. It was the same day Dave purchased 1,200 tickets for his road company of the Winfield Pavilion, so that New York kids could watch a doubleheader. And, in the third inning of the first game, he came to bat with the Mets ahead and two runners on base. His base hit scored both men and helped Gaylord Perry win the 276th game of his long career. Winfield surely must have thought back to Perry's remark about "not being aggressive enough" earlier in the season. Winfield would have been less than human if he didn't savor the moment just a mite more than usual.

For Winfield, the 1979 All-Star game was a reunion with three former college rivals, who had played against him in the 1973 College World Series game. Roy Smalley of the Minnesota Twins started at shortstop for the American League, Fred Lynn of the Boston Red Sox was in center, while Steve Kemp of the Detroit Tigers was an American League reserve. All three had played for USC.

"I remember that game well," Smalley said. "We got only one hit off Winfield going into the ninth and we trailed, 7-0. We scored eight runs to win, 8-7. Who could forget a game like that?"

Winfield made his contribution to the National League cause, getting a key hit in the rally that saw the Nationals win again, 7-5.

An interested spectator at the game was Walter Shannon, an executive with the Milwaukee Brewers organization. He commented on the fact that both Winfield and Paul Molitor, the Brewers infielder, had attended the University of Minnesota. They had actually grown up in the same section of St. Paul, perhaps a mile or so apart. With understandable bias, Shannon remarked, "Molitor in time may be the best player in the American League."

Molitor was then batting .326 for Milwaukee.

"And," Shannon continued, "Winfield is the best player in the National League."

Winfield was the second leading batter in his league at .325, with 22 home runs and 66 runs batted in.

By then Winfield had found his batting eye. The problem was the same one that had bedeviled him in the past, the hitch in the way he brought his bat around, dropping his hands before taking a full swing at the ball. He worked hard trying to get the proper rhythm as he cut at the ball, and finally he found the right groove.

As the season progressed, Winfield began to set his sights on three goals, all of which were within reach, provided he maintained the pace. His immediate target was the league's RBI crown. He was engaged in a battle with Mike Schmidt, and both were blistering the ball at an unbelievable pace. A July 23rd game was one indication of what happened when these two locked horns.

Schmidt drove in four runs during that game with a triple and his 34th home run, the latter count tops in the majors. Temporarily, he had the lead in RBIs with 75. He had 11 homers and 25 runs batted in over the previous 15 games.

Schmidt's lead lasted only until the seventh inning, when Winfield hit one out with a mate aboard, and in the ninth he singled with a man on second to drive in the winning tally. At game's end Winfield was still leading in RBIs, 77-75. It was a tribute to Winfield that he played at all. He had come to the ballpark with a bad summer cold, but evidently Philly pitching was better than a dose of penicillin.

Winfield's second goal was to win the league's Most Valuable Player award. And it was possible. Ostensibly, the award is given to the player who proves most valuable to his team, and if anyone was more precious to the Padres, no one knew his name.

Winfield solidified his claim to the honor when he bucked Atlanta pitching at the end of July. The Braves were his special pigeons, and that night he hit the jackpot. He slashed three singles, a double and his 25th home run to lead the Padres to a 10-3 laugher. He had also gotten three straight hits the previous game, giving him a run of eight consecutive safeties. The Braves could do nothing but leave the field muttering sourly. In 11 games against Atlanta, to that point, he had gone 21-for-38, including five homers and 17 runs batted in, for a sizzling .553 batting average.

Montreal was another team Winfield victimized. In a doubleheader he amassed four singles and two home runs in nine appearances at the plate, plus five runs batted in. He was making good his boast: "Put the men on the bases and I'll push them across."

However, Winfield could not continue such an all-out effort indefinitely and he began to tail off. As his average dipped he saw the MVP award slipping away, which in turn threatened his third goal, a new contract with a great increase in salary.

Winfield's contract extended only through 1980, after which he could become a free agent. Numerous teams were interested in him; during the All-Star game, Al Frohman had been seen talking to any number of baseball officials—"only a friendly chat," he would insist later, although those who knew Frohman had other opinions. Frohman reportedly told a broadcaster for the New York Mets that 1980 would be Winfield's last season in San Diego, because his client was going after the big bucks.

Nor was Winfield above the battle. He measured his own worth and compared himself favorably with the best hitters in both leagues. Asked about the possibility of signing with the Minnesota Twins when his San Diego contract ran out, he turned thumbs down emphatically.

"If they couldn't pay Rod Carew, they certainly can't pay me," he said. "I look for San Diego to make me an offer at the end of this year.... With the present free agent market, I feel that I will be paid more money than Carew."

Therefore, Winfield attached great importance to every time at bat, every base hit, every run batted in. Ball players feel that way even under normal circumstances, but Winfield was beginning to feel greater pressure daily. How he reacted was reported by the capable Bill Weurding, a San Diego sportswriter who also acted as official scorer for the Padres.

Late in the season, as Winfield's batting average began to fall to the .300 mark, the Padres played Los Angeles at home. Winfield hit a ball to Dodger third baseman Ron Cey, which Weurding ruled an error. That night Frohman called Weurding at home, asking that the entry be changed to a base hit.

"He asked that I do that because it was important to Dave that he hit over .300 and my call might kill his chances. He even suggested Winfield would never speak to me again if I didn't change my decision. I didn't yield to the pressure; our relationship (mine with both Frohman and Winfield) was a bit strained for many months after that...."

Some time later, learning of Weurding's statement, Winfield said in rebuttal, "The people in San Diego will say anything to make Al and me look bad. People will even take the pope and find something wrong with him. I'll tell you this: There's one team that's happy to have me. And the Yanks will be even happier when the year is over."

Winfield had any number of rivals for MVP honors in 1979, including such stalwarts as Willie Stargell of the Pirates, Bruce Sutter of the Cubs,

Keith Hernandez of the Cardinals, Steve Garvey of the Dodgers, and several others. He considered himself a legitimate contender, as indeed he was.

The Padres, meanwhile, had said repeatedly that they wanted to sign Winfield again, but in order to do that they had to convince Al Frohman, who did all the negotiating for his client.

It is difficult to figure out anyone's thinking process, especially when the stakes are high, but in Al Frohman's case a bit of conjecture might be fun, if not wholly accurate. Frohman was holding all the high cards in the deal and Ray Kroc was not even in a position to bluff, because his options were limited. In essence, Kroc had three choices:

First, he could throw up his hands at the end of the 1979 season and try to trade Winfield, who still had a year left on his contract. Some of the wealthier clubs might be interested, Los Angeles, for example, or the Yankees. They might deal some promising young players, plus perhaps a player of somewhat lesser status than Winfield, and take a chance that Winfield would sign a new contract. Such a deal was always a possibility. Actually, the Yankees secured Ken Griffey from the Cincinnati roster after the 1981 season by trading a young pitcher for Griffey, then signing him to a new contract. At the time, Griffey would have been in his option year with the Reds.

Second, Kroc could keep trying to retain Winfield by giving in and letting Winfield have his multimillion dollar deal. Admittedly it would be difficult to replace him, and just to substitute any warm body in right field would shortchange the fans. But, how much did Winfield want?

Third, Kroc could salvage one final year from Winfield and let him enter the free agent market without getting anything at all in return. There had to be a point of no return, and it appeared that Frohman and Winfield were determined to cross that barrier.

There was one slight hope for Kroc: that Winfield would tail off so badly near the end of the season that his value would be somewhat lessened. It had happened before, except for the 1978 season. A slumping Winfield might feel fan pressure to sign again.

Frohman, of course, was aware of all those possibilities. He also knew that the money specified in a player's contract is not the full story.

Winfield and Frohman both knew that. They could get money from any team, in generous quantities, but in San Diego, there was little possibility of sharing in the lucrative field of advertising endorsements. Yet if they sounded too mercenary, fans in *all* cities would sour on Winfield in spite of his foundation and community image.

Therefore, the skillful Frohman began to construct a minefield on the road to the negotiating table. He sounded the same old tune in the same old key.

"The big thing," Frohman said, "is what the team is going to be like. Is Dave going to get some help on the Padres? He has pride, he wants to play on a winner. If the Padres show him they will be going out to get quality players, then the chances of Dave's staying in San Diego are very good."

Frohman's statement was like an onion in that it had many layers to be peeled away before getting to the nub of it. The nitty-gritty was that Frohman was telling Kroc how to run his baseball team if he wanted to keep Winfield in the fold. He would have had better results using a cattle prod on the hamburger monarch, who was old enough to be set in his ways, and successful enough to do exactly as he chose.

Kroc did promise to try to improve the team, but he would have promised the same thing to any bleacher fan who paid his hard-earned dollars to watch his beloved losers. Has there ever been an athletic organization which did not try to do better next time? Kroc didn't want a loser any more than Frohman or Winfield did.

So it was a temporary Mexican standoff. Frohman had to issue periodic communiques to the effect that Winfield did really want to stay in San Diego under the proper conditions, while Kroc had to signal that he was ready to negotiate in good faith at any time. Perhaps it is hindsight to indicate that both parties knew the eventual outcome, but all the signs were there to be read. A little study of Frohman's psychological warfare might have helped too.

By the end of the season Winfield had attained one of his objectives, lost out on the second, and left the third in limbo. He did win the runs batted in crown in the National League, with 118. The rest of the stats were outstanding for this big man: a .308 batting average for the second successive year, with 34 home runs, 10 triples, 27 doubles, 97 runs scored, 15 stolen bases, 184 hits, 85 bases on balls. Those were truly superstar stats, considering the fact that he was playing on a fifth place ball club.

There was no question in Dave Winfield's mind that he should be the league's Most Valuable Player. The fans in San Diego thought so, and so did many sports writers throughout the land, including the baseball writers whose votes counted toward the award. Unfortunately for Winfield, not enough of the latter thought so. Two players were tied for first place in the ballot: Willie Stargell, the great star of the champion Pittsburgh Pirates and Keith Hernandez of the St. Louis Cardinals. Each received 216 points. Winfield trailed with 155 points.

Dave's disappointment was etched on his face. "I was a distant third, and that was a bit surprising," he said. "But I wouldn't trade my year for anybody's."

Later, Winfield was able to place the entire situation in its proper perspective. "I can't lament something I never had," he commented. "Of course the Padres didn't do too well as a team [the Padres finished fifth, 22 games out], and perhaps my input wasn't evaluated accordingly. I think if the Padres had been in contention for the pennant, my chances would have been much better."

Jerry Coleman, the former Yankees second baseman and broadcaster of the Padres games, who was to manage San Diego in 1980, remarked, "If Dave had been on a better team he would have won it this year. But people are going to look at him and say, 'Well, his team finished fifth, so he couldn't have done too much.' All I can say is, I hate to think what this team would have done without him."

Ballard Smith, president of the ball club, was another who thought Winfield had been done out of the MVP award. "I've already said publicly that I think Dave is the most valuable player in the National League. I've told him that privately, too, even though we're trying to negotiate a new contract with him, and that's not going to make it any easier."

No, it wasn't easy. In fact, it turned out to be just about impossible.

11

What a Kroc!

"I didn't ask to be captain. Maybe we'll take another look at that next spring. Maybe they'll appoint somebody else captain and that will motivate him to hit .310."

The statement was made by Dave Winfield at the close of the 1979 season, in response to manager Roger Craig's remark that he had appointed Winfield captain of the Padres as a device to motivate him. During the season some of his teammates had wondered aloud whether Winfield was deserving of the honor. Gene Tenace, they alleged, was the team's real leader.

Winfield tried to remain above the criticism. "I'd like to avoid being controversial. This business about me not being a good captain takes me through so many kinds of emotions. I have tried to lead by example. I thought I had a pretty good season. But I don't socialize with the other players, I don't hang out with the guys. Does it make you a good captain if you buy a round of drinks?"

Nor would he jump all over the recently discharged Roger Craig for his remark about naming him captain for motivation purposes. Some of the players had taken advantage of Craig, whose generous nature made him look like a patsy at times.

"Roger did the best he could with what he had," was Winfield's analysis. "You may remember that during spring training, when everybody was predicting great things, I said that at best we would be exciting. I couldn't see we had made much improvement. But I'm not going to sit back and complain."

As for the new manager, Jerry Coleman, Winfield allowed as how he was perfectly willing to give him the benefit of the doubt. It was to be Coleman's maiden effort as the skipper of a baseball team. In fact he had never even been a coach. His other credentials, however, were impeccable.

As a member of the New York Yankees infield, Coleman had been a decent enough hitter, but as a fielder he was absolutely tops. No less an observer than Casey Stengel had said of him, "That feller Coleman turns over the double play better'n any second baseman I ever saw. He takes the relay an' bang!—he gets rid of it. All the kids should study him to see how it's done."

Coleman broke into the majors in 1949 and was voted Rookie of the Year by the Associated Press. Tall, slender, graceful, Coleman could cover ground, had a good arm, and came up with clutch hits. He was with the Yankees in eight of their pennant years and in six World Series. The two he missed were indicative of his youth and courage.

Jerry had been a pilot during World War II. With the outbreak of hostilities in Korea, he was summoned back to the service and what he did was the stuff story books are made of. He flew 120 missions, winning two Distinguished Flying Crosses, 13 Air Medals, and three Navy Citations, emerging as a lieutenant colonel in the United States Marines. However, that surprised no one who knew him. He was an outstanding ball player and an equally outstanding American.

After hanging up his spikes, Coleman served for two seasons as the Yankees' personnel director, during which time he supervised the signing of such players as Joe Pepitone, Jim Bouton, and Tom Tresh. Then he worked in the media as one of the Yankees announcers for seven years, transferring over to the Padres later on.

Coleman had certainly played enough baseball, seen enough baseball, and observed enough strategy to write his own textbook if he wanted to second guess anybody. And he also knew the value of a good outfielder. He had, after all, been one of Joe DiMaggio's teammates during the Yankee Clipper's twilight years in the game, and he had seen the rise of another pretty fair ball-hawk named Mickey Mantle. Coleman told the press right off what he thought of Dave Winfield:

"I hope the San Diego management and Dave Winfield can get together on a new contract, because Winfield is a super player."

By then the skirmishing had been in progress for some months. Contract negotiations had bogged down and in its place a war of nerves was raging between Ballard Smith and Al Frohman. While it stopped short of violence, there seemed to be everything else which could be used as a weapon, including namecalling, innuendo, and all sorts of accusations.

"Al Frohman is not one of my favorite people," said Smith. "I feel if I could just sit down with Dave alone, we would have a chance to work this thing out."

"I'm not real fond of Ballard either," riposted Al Frohman, "but personalities shouldn't enter into this thing. In business you often have to deal with people you don't particularly like. I'll tell you this—if Ballard thinks he can avoid me and still have a chance at signing Winfield, let him try. It isn't going to happen."

Ballard Smith had made Winfield-Frohman an offer which he deemed more than generous. It was a six-year contract calling for a base salary of $500,000 a year, and filled with a series of incentive clauses, all of them in six figures. If Dave made the All-Star team, he'd receive an added $100,000. If he won the Gold Glove Award for fielding, another $100,000 would be added. Similar numbers were on tap for being chosen MVP and for leading the league in runs batted in or other categories. There were attendance incentives as well.

Al Frohman called the offer "insulting." He said Winfield was insulted too. Winfield put in, "I scoffed at it. It hurt. I'm not going to worry about it, though. I', staying out of this thing and just concentrating on playing baseball. I don't want to be distracted or harassed."

Frohman made use of his favorite ploy, asking a rhetorical question and answering it himself.

"What's the first thing you do if you have a Cadillac you want to sell? Obviously, what you do first is determine its market value. Then you sell it for that price, not a third or a half of that price."

He added, "I know one thing, $500,000 is not Winfield's market value. He could go play for the Timbuctu [team] for $500,000."

Frohman's implications were fairly clear. If $500,000 was one third or one half of Winfield's value, then he was thinking in terms of $1 million to $1.5 million per year, and certainly a contract for at least a five-year term.

No doubt the average fan had some difficulty grasping the numbers being tossed back and forth with such careless abandon, but even some simple arithmetic and the use of a pencil could clarify everything. Mr. Bleacherite, who was trying to support his wife and kids on less than $20,000 a year, was reading about an outraged baseball player who demanded at least $20,000 *per week*!

Yet Frohman was not really out of line, considering the insanely inflated salaries in professional sports. Winfield would play every day; Nolan Ryan, a pitcher who might play every fourth day, was getting $1 million a year. Using such logic, Winfield's asking price was relatively low.

The Al Frohman-Ballard Smith "debate" became juicy copy as they traded personal barbs. Reporters hung around, eagerly waiting for the lunge-and-parry of the day, and it was all dutifully reported.

Frohman, quoted in the *Sporting News*: "Ballard Smith? He couldn't get any job on the club if his father-in-law didn't own it."

Smith, to anyone who would listen: "I'm tired of Al Frohman. The guy's insulting. I'll stand on what I've done. I don't know what he's done. This is the one big chance in his lifetime to get his name in the paper and see himself on TV. Frohman told me that the Yankees and the Montreal Expos were inquiring about Winfield, and what was happening with his contract."

Frohman: "It's a lie. It's a dream. It's a figment of Smith's imagination. Let him quote himself."

Smith: "Why should I make that up? He told those things to me."

Frohman: "He forgets things. His memory is only for an hour. He forgot what he promised Winfield for being captain."

Actually, the whole thing was funnier than a Marx Brothers movie with Groucho and Chico trading insults. But there was a serious note underlying all the comic banter, and that was, where did the owner draw the line? Even in the modern credit card economy, wasn't there some limit beyond which Kroc could no longer use his Mastercard?

Ballard Smith had stated for the record that the Padres lost $600,000 in 1979, a figure quickly challenged by Frohman. In a fit of pique Smith released to the *Los Angeles Times* the Padres' schedule of cash flow for fiscal 1979, which ended on October 31st of that year.

The list showed income of $8,110,730 and expenses of $8,561,164, indicating a loss of $470,434. The budget had been based on total attendance of 1.45 million fans for the year. For 1980, Smith estimated a loss of $1 million, based on attendance of 1.5 million. The Padres had paid out $2,798,289 for players' salaries in 1979, and the 1980 figure would be around $3.7 million.

"And that's pure, unadulterated salaries, that's not talking about bonuses," Smith pointed out. "We haven't broken even since the reentry draft started after the 1976 season."

Smith confessed that the Padres had been as guilty as any club in helping to inflate salaries. "We got involved to the tune of a couple of million dollars with Rollie Fingers and Gene Tenace and we stayed involved with Oscar Gamble. We stayed out for a year and then we got back involved with Rick Wise and John Curtis."

Times readers received an education in the economics of running a baseball team from Ballard Smith. For instance, there was no big television bonanza for the Padres.

"The Yankees get $5 million for local TV alone," he said. "That's more than seven times what we get for local TV. We can never hope to close that gap because TV money is based on population, and they have that huge market. We don't have that kind of population in San Diego."

As for promotional gimmicks which often sold out the ballpark, Smith cited facts which proved that numbers could be deceiving.

"Let's look at our Cap Night," Smith offered. "We have a full house and give away 50,000 caps. Last year the caps cost $1.25 each. Take a two-dollar general admission ticket for example. We pay 8 percent to the city, that's 16 cents. The visiting club and the league get 49 cents.

Counting the caps, that's $1.90. We have 20,000 general admission seats. How much profit is that?"

Why then didn't the Padres raise the price of admission? "We're trying to keep ticket prices down," Smith explained. "We've got the lowest ticket prices in baseball. We didn't raise them, and maybe we should have, but I didn't feel we could raise them after the team had performed so poorly."

Early in March Al Frohman handed in what was presumed to be the demands San Diego had to meet in order for Winfield to sign a new contract. Since the Padres had made an offer, Frohman could do no less than make a counteroffer. In all likelihood Frohman must have expected several of his proposals to be tossed out, for to have met them would have been total insanity:

Winfield was to receive $1.3 million as a base annual salary.
If the Padres moved their franchise out of San Diego, his contract would be voided.
Winfield must have the right of approval before the club could be sold.
Ray Kroc had to guarantee the contract, personally and with his estate.

There were several additional proposals Frohman wanted considered:

A million-dollar bonus for signing the contract.
Free agency for Winfield if the Padres were sold, or if ownership changed hands.
A deferral of payment beyond the ten years of the contract, and partial compensation in the form of a McDonald's fast-food franchise.

"Dave wants all the guarantees and offers us none," Ballard Smith noted. "But deep down I still believe we're going to sign him. I can't really explain it, maybe it's just wishful thinking, but I have hopes it's going to work out."

Ray Kroc wasn't that optimistic. "If a fellow can make a fortune somewhere else, let him go ahead. I can't necessarily do it for him."

Kroc was beginning to sour on baseball completely. "When I got into baseball," he said, "I thought it was a good investment. Now I know better."

Asked to comment about the $500,000 the Padres had initially offered Winfield, Kroc laughed, "Hellfire, I never made $350,000 a year."

Meanwhile, more of Frohman's demands were surfacing. Of Dave's salary, 15 percent was to go to the David Winfield Foundation. The club was to give an additional $10,000 to the foundation in the event they ended the season with a division championship.

By the second week in March Ballard Smith was ready to toss out all the negotiations. "Maybe it's best we just forget the whole thing for a while and let Dave concentrate on playing baseball," he said. "We're not close in the negotiations and I really can't see us getting any closer."

Ray Kroc put in, "If Frohman wants to run the club, let him buy it."

Joan Kroc, Ray's wife and a member of the San Diego board, was more vehement. "We'll agree to those terms over my dead body," she said. "It's ridiculous. The only thing Frohman hasn't asked for is the Padres plane. No, on second thought, he also forgot the Big Mac bus and the McDonald helicopter."

After calming down a bit she added, "I feel bad about this. I admire Dave. I think he's a fine athlete and a fine young man. But I have to question whether he's getting good advice."

Meanwhile, Ballard Smith had taken it upon himself to release to the press the demands Frohman had made. It was not a wise move on his part, and he admitted as much later, but if any defense of his action was possible, perhaps he thought that since he had been open about the Padres' offer to Winfield, why couldn't Frohman's counteroffer also be made public? In most negotiations, this is considered a no-no. Frohman had reason to be highly exercised.

"They're using the media to influence public opinion," he charged, "instead of studying the proposals and making other proposals."

Jerry Coleman, the new manager, seemed to be caught in the middle of the controversy and did his best to calm the troubled waters by naming Winfield captain of the team again. Winfield accepted the post with an explanation of his actions the previous year.

"I don't like losing," he said. "I just can't handle it. That's why, last year when we were losing so much, I concentrated on individual goals and everything started coming out 'I' instead of 'We.' I'm sure the guys didn't like that. Also, because of my outside activities in the community, everything was 'Winfield,' 'Winfield.' I'm hoping to get more of our players involved in some of the things I've been doing, and I think you'll see it happen."

Winfield was also trying to show the Padres that he was a team man. "I had six players down to my room the other night, and we all sat around and talked baseball for hours. Believe me, this has never happened before. I don't make predictions, but I do feel we have the makings of a much better ball club this year."

The Padres, like all teams, had not stood pat with their roster, especially in view of a losing season. They had acquired Willie Montanez, a much-traveled first baseman who hit with occasional power and was an adequate fielder; they also got infielders Dave Cash and Aurelio Rodriguez, the latter a veteran who couldn't hit much but was a stone wall around third base.

However, Winfield began to see and to personally feel the damaging effects of the contract controversy in the first exhibition game of the season, against the Oakland Athletics. Almost 4,500 patrons were on hand in Desert Sun Stadium, a big crowd by Cactus League standards. As the San Diego players were introduced the spectators responded with some hand clapping, a cheer or two, until Dave Winfield's name was announced. Instead of the roar that always greeted him, he was met with a wave of hoots, jeers, and boos which continued through most of the game.

Dave was stung badly but his face remained impassive. "They always boo me on the road," he quipped, trying to make light of his true feelings, but then he added, more soberly, "Nobody likes it but it's part of the game."

Later, however, he got a few things off his chest. "The front office says almost all the people who have written or phoned them about my contract negotiations are against me. That's strange. The people I'm hearing from are urging me to hang in there."

He got in a few licks of his own about the Padres and their financial condition. "They're saying they'll have to raise ticket prices if they give me what I'm asking. They are going to raise them whether they sign me or not. They told me that last weekend, they would have raised the prices this winter if the team hadn't played so poorly last season. I have that on a tape recorder."

On March 22nd, *The Daily Californian,* a local newspaper in East San Diego County, published a particularly vitriolic attack on Winfield. The paper had previously published a "ballot" of sorts pertaining to Winfield's contract and asked the fans for their opinions on a "would give" or "would not give" basis. Exactly 195 responses were tallied, hardly sufficient to be regarded as a statistically representative poll. A gentleman named Dave Hatz, evidently a staff writer according to his byline, chided Winfield. In his column, "The Fans Speak," Mr. Hatz wrote:

"To put it mildly, Mr. David Mark Winfield, you're no longer Mr. Popular in San Diego. Remember those boos you heard in Yuma last week? Well, you can expect them to be magnified by several hundred decibels if and when the Padres play in the stadium this spring, and they will continue all season long.

"East County baseball fans—maybe we should make that ex-fans where Winfield is concerned—were given a chance to voice their opinions through a ballot listing the All-Star outfielder's desires for a new pact to replace the one that expires at the end of the approaching season.

"An overwhelming majority of the 195 people who responded are opposed to the Padres fulfilling any of his wishes.

"And many of the fans weren't content just to cast their votes. Plenty of [comments] concerning his demands were made, and here is just a sample."

Regarding the $1.3 million annual salary for a full decade, with Winfield donating 15 percent ($195,000) to the foundation, 186 fans said they would not give Winfield that much money, only 9 would. As for the annual cost of living increase, the vote was 172-19 against, with 4 giving no response. The increase depending on attendance, the signing bonus, the performance considerations—all the questions—received the same fan reaction, which was overwhelmingly negative.

Cutting Winfield even more deeply was the sampling of gratuitous remarks reportedly made by fans. The first three or four were more or less on Dave's side, the rest were taunts, brickbats, insults:

"Pay Winfield what he wants now or lose him to another team that will. After all, in three or four years $1.3 million won't be that high."

"Every team needs a star and we sure need Winfield. I hope the Padres are willing to meet him halfway."

"Pay him $1 more than Dave Parker."

"$750,000 a year for 10 years with a 6 percent cost of living increase. That's it. The rest of his demands are absurd."

Those were the good ones. There were twenty-eight others. To cite a few:

"I'd rather have a losing ball club than a prima donna."

"Kroc should tell Winfield where to go and to take his flunky agent with him."

"Is Al Frohman trying to ruin all of baseball or just Dave Winfield?"

"Greed will kill sports as surely as it is wrecking the economy of this country unless something is done to arrest the gluttonous appetites of the superstars."

"If Winfield gets this contract I'll never again attend another Padres game."

"This is a public holdup."

"No one walks on water, not even Dave Winfield."

"Sit on it, Winfield!"

"We should trade him for a couple of good water boys. He cannot compare to Dave Parker, but the media has convinced him he is as good."

"San Diego fans made Dave Winfield a superstar. They went out of their way to put him in the All-Star game. He is an egotistical mediocre ballplayer who needs the Padres more than they need him."

"I work 60 hours a week just to pay my bills and put food on the table. Ask me an intelligent question."

"Put him in a chicken suit and let him make some extra money that way."

"After reading this incredible set of demands I think he must have been standing in the sun too long."

Was that "poll" paid for or inspired by the San Diego brass? It was possible to get an opinion either way. The reaction from Frohman and Winfield was typical of both.

"Negotiations belong in a place where you can negotiate, not in tirades before fans," Frohman snapped angrily.

Winfield was more philosophical; in fact he was almost clairvoyant when he said, "If I play well I'll be a hero. The boos change to cheers when you hit a triple in the first inning. And there will be plenty of them this year."

In the first inning of the season's opener against San Francisco, Winfield came to bat with two Padres on base. As Winfield predicted, he was greeted with booing, mixed with a smattering of cheers. Then he lashed one to left center driving in both runners, and maybe he tried to make the whole thing come true because he tried for third and was out. It was almost as if Winfield were reenacting Babe Ruth's historic shot in the 1932 World Series when he indicated his home run into the center field bleachers. Dave was right; the crowd gave him a standing ovation. The Padres won that one.

The cheers continued in a subsequent 4-2 victory over the same Giants. Winfield drove home all four runs with a two-run single and a home run with a man on base. If there were any nay-sayers in the stands they were not in evidence, but there were some indications of disenchantment by some of the advertisers who thought even a giveaway featuring the outfielder might be unpopular.

The Central Federal Savings & Loan Co. had agreed to distribute some 16,000 tote bags with Winfield's picture on them. Such stencils take time, and meanwhile Winfield seemed to have fallen from grace with the fans. Therefore the bank had the Padres' logo placed on the tote bags instead. They had not reckoned on Dave's hitting. The fans even applauded when Dave struck out after his single and homer.

Winfield, the previous season's RBI leader, had already driven in seven runs in three games, and refused to become ruffled over the change on the tote bags.

"There is change in everything. They can't get me down over something involving tote bags," he said. "I'm playing for this club. I appreciate the guys we have on this team."

The euphoria began to wane soon enough. The Padres lost the finale of the four-game series with the Giants, 3-1, due in part to a Winfield error. The score was tied at 1-all, and on a hit-and-run play, Rennie Stennett lit out for second base. Milt May, the batter, lifted a routine fly to right field near the foul line. Winfield dropped it, the run scored, and it proved to be the winning tally.

"I have no excuse," said the subdued Winfield. "I knew I had Rennie doubled off first base and I took my eye off the ball for a second."

The Padres—and Winfield—went right down the tube. On their first road trip of the year they lost nine of ten, falling to fifth place, a half-game out of the cellar. Winfield was hitting .241 when the Padres returned home and unpacked their bags. The rest of the team was mired in the same slump.

Yet, as often as not he got good wood on the ball, but with negative results. In a game against the Braves, Dave came up in the fifth inning with the bases loaded and two out. He belted one to center, and Brian Asseltine made a diving catch to retire the side. In the seventh, with two on, he smashed a line drive right at shortstop Larvell Blanks.

"I'm not worried, I'm okay," Winfield insisted. "The hits will start to fall for me. We've only played a small segment of the season. I'll probably go through a period where I get a lot of cheap hits and RBIs. Lately I haven't had anything go my way."

Sportswriter Bill Weurding did some homework and came up with an amazing statistic regarding Winfield's slump. Although it was not reflected in his batting average, Dave was following the previous season's pace in both home runs and runs batted in. Only one eighth of the season had elapsed, and Winfield already had four homers and 15 RBIs.

Furthermore, Weurding's statistics proved that Winfield was absolutely correct when he kept saying he hit best with runners on base—at least to that point at the beginning of May. He was hitting .303 with runners on base and .156 when he batted with the bases empty. So, if the Padres were losing, much of the blame had to be shouldered by those batting ahead of Winfield. They weren't getting on base and he became disheartened.

Winfield must have realized what was going on, and perhaps he was loath to criticize his teammates, except with a slap at himself, and by letting the fans draw their own conclusions.

"To do what I did last year was impossible," he said, alluding to his 118

RBIs. "Now, maybe people have come to expect that from me. Maybe people look at what I did as commonplace, but it isn't. I did the impossible last year and you shouldn't expect that every year."

It was apparent that Winfield was becoming tense and more nervous as the season continued. He got into hot water for bumping an umpire, and in a midseason game against the Astros he was thrown out of the game after taking a couple of punches at pitcher Nolan Ryan. In all fairness the incident was nobody's fault. Ryan, in the six innings he pitched, was scatter-armed. He walked four and hit the weak-hitting Ozzie Smith with a pitch, a sure indication that he was having trouble locating his pitches. Pitching to Winfield in the fourth, he threw a high inside blazer which decked the batter, and two pitches later Ryan threw another. Winfield rushed the mound, and both benches emptied.

"That was too many pitches too close to my head," said Winfield. "Part of what is going on has to do with intimidation. Some teams throw at me more than others. I have to protect myself."

Fair enough. Ryan's explanation was also reasonable.

"I don't think I have to apologize for what happened," the pitcher countered. "The Padres didn't say anything about all the people I walked. It's getting to where you can't pitch anyone on the inside of the plate without them thinking you're throwing at them. A lot of hitters are charging the mound this year. I don't understand it."

Winfield, meanwhile, was acting out the old adage, "When you're hot, you're hot, and when you're not, you're not." In the past he had wreaked havoc with Montreal pitching, but one game against the Expos had to rank among the longest nights ever experienced by any baseball player, past or present.

In the first inning, with a runner in scoring position, Dave bounced out to the infield. In the third, with a runner on first, he got the hit-and-run sign. Dave didn't swing and the runner was out by a mile. In the fifth, with the bases loaded, he struck out swinging on a bad pitch. In the ninth, again with the bases loaded, Dave took a called third strike. Thus he had left seven runners on base and was directly responsible for erasing another from the paths.

Winfield had to be honest, especially about the sign he disobeyed. "I got the sign and I meant to swing," he said, "but then I got a curve ball that started up and in on me and I just couldn't swing. I just lost my concentration, I guess."

But it was a poor excuse at best. Even a handcuffed Winfield should have swung through the pitch, if only to distract the catcher momentarily.

Jerry Coleman could only commiserate. "It's a shame," he moaned, "because you can see him up there bearing down and trying. It just isn't happening for him. I think the pressure and all this publicity is haunting him."

Yet the same pressure-packed Winfield could deliver in the clutch sometimes. Like the game against Pittsburgh, when he came off the bench and pinch-hit a home run to ignite the winning rally. For the bewildered outfielder, 1980 was a season-long nightmare, like an accident waiting to happen.

As Winfield floundered, Ballard Smith's position grew stronger, but sometimes he seemed to contradict himself. On the one hand he would say, "I can't tell you how I've agonized over Dave. I know he is the best player ever to wear a San Diego uniform. But this controversy is having a psychological affect on him and on the rest of the team."

On the other hand he would say to a reporter, "If Dave Winfield were playing up to his potential, the Padres would be over .500 now. I think that's fairly obvious. Naturally we're concerned about him. These should be his peak years and you have every right to expect a player to be improving every season at his age."

Then, thinking of the million-plus Dave wanted, Smith sighed, "It would sure be easier paying what he demands if he were playing like he deserves it."

Printing statements like that, the San Diego sportswriters seemed to be saying their goodbyes early to Winfield. Some baseball "experts," however, seemed convinced that Dave would stay in San Diego. Buzzie Bavasi, who had gone around and around with Frohman during his tenure with the Padres, thought the outfielder would stay put at a price the Padres could afford.

"Loyalty," Bavasi pontificated, "is important to Dave. I'm talking about loyalty to San Diego, I don't mean loyalty to the club. Dave feels strongly about the people of San Diego. I'm sure he doesn't want to leave."

Coleman, meanwhile, was burning the midnight oil trying to devise some method that would lift the Padres from the doldrums. He recalled that shifting Winfield from clean-up to third in the batting order had done wonders for him before, and he juggled the lineup again, moving Winfield up a notch.

"We haven't really had a number-3 hitter all year," Coleman explained, "and David hasn't been hitting like a number-4 hitter anyway, so I figured, what can it hurt?"

On June 23rd, for a game against the Pirates, Coleman started his revamped batting order. Winfield responded. In the first inning he came to bat with two mates aboard and lofted his seventh home run of the season. It was his first four-master since May 30th, when he hit a solo homer against Cincinnati.

In the second inning Winfield's sacrifice fly scored the runner from third, and in the eighth he tripled home Ozzie Smith, to round out a very productive five-RBI game.

"Last year, about this time, the same thing was tried," Dave remembered. "Batting third I went on a tear for a while, and I hope it happens again. I need only a few games like this to move from a mediocre year to a good one."

A week later Winfield drove in three runs as the Padres beat the Dodgers, 4-1. In the first inning, with runners on second and third, his groundout produced a score, and in the third, with one on, Winfield creamed a rising line drive that went out of the park like a shot, directly over the center field fence.

It was very difficult to be a Padres fan as summer settled over the land. The great contract dispute had degenerated into a series of traded recriminations, like two opposing snipers taking verbal potshots at each other. The lead sports item in the *San Diego Union* on July 12th was indicative of what the fans had to endure when they read their daily baseball report. It was like reading about one's family, most of them losers, engaging in a series of tiresome tirades.

The headline read, "Padres Lose Seventh Straight, Winfield Appears 'Gone.'" The featured photograph showed Ozzie Smith being tagged out after being caught off base by pitcher Ed Whitson's pickoff throw. Staff writer Phil Collier quoted pitcher Randy Smith: "I have a gut feeling Winfield will be leaving."

Ballard Smith was present at the 7-3 loss, and he criticized Winfield for his failure to hustle down to first in the seventh inning, claiming he could have beaten out the grounder for an infield hit and kept the two-run rally alive.

At the time Winfield had raised his stats considerably. He was batting a healthy .302, with nine home runs and 55 RBIs. In the recently played All-Star game, he had driven in what proved to be the winning run. He had every reason to snap back at the San Diego management, particularly because they had failed to nominate him for the National League's "star of the week."

During that previous week's stretch of seven games, Winfield had gone 14-for-30 (.467) with two homers and 10 runs batted in.

"It would be tough for anybody to have a better week than that," Winfield declared, not unreasonably, "and they didn't even bother to submit my name for the All-Star game."

The Padres public relations director Bob Chandler replied with the excuse that the failure to nominate Winfield was purely an oversight, to which Dave replied, "In my own mind I know the front office didn't want me to make the All-Star team."

There were a couple more sporadic, desultory, totally futile attempts at negotiating sessions, and the die was cast when *Sports Illustrated* printed an interview with Ray Kroc in its August 11th issue. It was a most revealing article, for it showed that the San Diego front office was in disarray, both before and after Kroc purchased the team.

For instance, before Kroc took over, general manager Buzzie Bavasi wanted to sign Doug DeCinces; but the previous owner would only part with $4,000, while DeCinces wanted $6,000. The Padres passed up the draft rights to George Brett because they didn't think they could afford him. They did draft Warren Cromartie and Bump Wills, a pair of quality young players, but couldn't sign them. Evidently the previous owner was on some sort of ill-advised economy drive.

Kroc hardly improved the situation, but his improvidences were of a different nature. He parted with some $10 million chasing free agents, such as Rollie Fingers, Gene Tenace, outfielder Oscar Gamble, pitchers John Curtis and Rick Wise, and with the exception of Fingers (he eventually lost Fingers through subsequent free agency) none of them was worth the money.

Oscar Gamble was a case in point. In 1978 the San Diego outfield seemed all set with Winfield in right; George Hendrick, a proven hitter in center; and young Gene Richards in left. Gamble had a super year in 1977 with the White Sox, clouting 31 home runs and batting in 87 runs. San Diego gave Gamble financial security into middle age, by signing him to a contract calling for a $150,000 bonus, $200,000 for six years, then $100,000 a year for the next 15 years, to 1998. It was, in short, a *twenty-one-year deal,* totalling $2.85 million (and if that doesn't explain Winfield's demands, what can?).

Having secured Gamble, a new problem arose: where to put him. He was an outfielder by trade and the National League still has no truck with designated hitters, so Gamble had to play in the outer gardens— otherwise the Padres would have signed the most expensive pinch hitter in history. Gene Richards was shifted to first base, which he handled with absolutely no distinction. Pitcher Bob Owchinko observed Richards and commented, "He can't pick up a ball until it stops rolling." That wasn't Richards' fault. He never claimed he was a first baseman.

If Gamble had produced, the Padres would have saved face, but he didn't. Those 17-foot walls loomed like the Alps, and Gamble had only seven home runs with 47 RBIs. The Padres gave up on Gamble and traded him to Texas for Mike Hargrove, who had always hit well. But he didn't in San Diego.

Kroc let his ego override his good sense with Dave Kingman and George Hendrick. Kingman liked the good life in San Diego and offered to sign a five-year contract. Kroc disapproved of the way Kingman dressed and his supposed lack of hustle, so he packed him off at the $20,000 waiver price. Hendrick was a loner who refused to talk to reporters, which miffed Kroc. When the outfielder failed to show up at a testimonial dinner in Kroc's honor, he was traded to St. Louis for pitcher Eric Rasmussen. Hendrick bombed enemy pitching in his new Cardinals uniform, while at midseason of 1980, Rasmussen was 2-8 with an earned run average of 5.15.

Kroc's disillusionment with America's National Pastime was freely expressed in the *Sports Illustrated* piece. Early in August the team was fifth, ten and a half games behind, ten games under the .500 mark (they would finish sixth, nineteen and a half games behind, sixteen games under .500) and the fast-food financier was not in a jovial mood. The big story was still Winfield, and Kroc opened up the floodgates, beginning with the cost of living clause Frohman wanted to insert in the contract.

"Cost of living?" grated the boss. "He wants a million-three *plus* a cost of living? Plus a Cadillac, plus, plus, plus, plus, plus . . . I don't want him here at any price. A million-three! Who's going to pay him? I'm not going to pay him. The customers aren't going to pay him. We had 11,000 here last night. I'm going to lose between $2 million and $3 million this year. Let somebody else have him. I don't want him."

Winfield let go with his own salvo. "I've been here eight years, and we've had eight different face-lifts of the team," he said. "We've had two different owners, three different general managers, five different managers . . . we've no identity or tradition. We even had a different uniform every year."

It is conceivable that Winfield might have kept his cool were it not for the growing chorus of boos that greeted him on the home field. Yet, in early July he was once again considered Mr. Nice Guy and everybody loved him because of his unswerving devotion to "his kids." His annual All-Star party, at the Elysian Park Recreation Center, located near Dodger Stadium in Los Angeles, was bigger and better than ever.

For this affair Winfield inaugurated a new idea in the form of a fancy acronym, HOPE—the letters meaning Health Optimization Planning and Education. It was a kind of "clinic," in conjunction with the Scripps Research Foundation.

"We'll be working with doctors and technicians," Dave had said, "dealing with things like weight, height, pulse, exercise, diet, and nutrition. All the things kids and parents have to think about to stay healthy."

More than forty nonpaid Scripps and Winfield Foundation volunteers came to the Elysian Recreation Center to work with a mob of youngsters estimated to number between 20,000 and 30,000. Winfield was there, of course, and so were a number of other players, including Von Joshua, Tim Flannery, Kurt Bevacqua, and Steve Swisher. The first order of business seemed to be collecting autographs; then came the physical examinations at the various health stations that had been set up, followed by hot dogs and milk. Afterward came the ball game.

The physical checkups were not routine. Of the first 53 kids examined, one boy was discovered to have an irregular heartbeat, two had dangerously high blood pressure, and several, according to Dr. Gary Sherer, the executive director of preventive medicine at Scripps, needed further medical examination and attention as soon as practicable.

However, the fans seemed to be looking at two Dave Winfields, one the man who helped kids and the other a baseball player asking for the moon. They seemed intent on separating one from the other, cheering him because of his humanitarian instincts and voicing displeasure at his contractual demands. The great love affair between Winfield and the San Diego patrons had disintegrated, like a marriage that had begun filled with roses and had seen the flowers die, with only the thorns left. A divorce was inevitable.

"It feels here [in San Diego] like I'm on the road, like I'm the enemy," Winfield told Al Frohman. Dave had always drawn sustenance from cheers and approval. Now he was a starving man.

Winfield could find respite only on the road, where he was just another visiting ball player doing his job. On a late August eight-game trip he vented his feelings by abusing opposing pitchers with his bat, going 13-for-35 (.371), with five homers and nine RBIs. Back at Jack Murphy Stadium he was almost helpless at the plate and became an automatic out. In the contests following that road trip he had a mere seven hits in 34 trips to the plate (.206) with no home runs and exactly one run batted in. During one interval he failed to get the ball out of the infield in 15 consecutive times at bat.

If it was any consolation to Winfield, Dave Parker of the Pirates, the player he was usually compared to, was also enduring the hostility of his Pittsburgh fans, the only difference being that Parker had signed a contract calling for $900,000 a year. Winfield still had nothing.

Frohman seemed to be having second thoughts about the hornets" nest he had stirred up. "If I had it to do all over again, I'd never have made those suggestions, believe me," he remarked ruefully. "That negotiating thing has been the biggest problem. It turned the fans against Dave from the beginning. The fans have a right to boo Winfield this year. He's not performing the way he should. But I think what is bothering Dave is that they started booing so early, long before this slump."

Even Frohman's confidence seemed to have been shaken by this long summer of discontent. In the past he had exuded certainty: "There's no doubt about it, he'll get $1 million-plus."

Jerry Coleman, summing up Dave Winfield's situation, with respect to his contract and the year he was having at bat and in the field, said, "It has to be a difficult thing, I don't care who you are. He has had his contract negotiations in the papers, and that can't help.

"He has been booed by the fans in his own home town and that has to be rough. And he has been a busy man with all his outside activities which, I'm sure, has taken a lot of time and drained him. You may play baseball only three hours a day but it's a job that requires 24 hours of your concentration. There comes a time when a guy has to stop, look around, and simply ask himself, 'hey, what's my job?'"

Jerry Coleman was full of admiration for what Dave was doing for the kids all over the country, but he was also sure that these activities of Dave's had affected his game both physically and mentally.

Dave Winfield didn't agree with Coleman, not at all.

"My outside activities," said Dave, "have given me some of my best years in baseball. My work in the community doesn't take from me. On the contrary, it has kept me going during all the seasons when our ball club hasn't had that much going of a positive nature on the field."

Cynics may scoff at this sort of statement, and suggest some egotistical and selfish motive was behind all the good deeds of David Winfield. It certainly is true that Dave Winfield was always concerned with his image, that more than anything else he wanted respect and even love, but facts are facts, and the principal fact is that Dave gave much of himself, and more than most, for the welfare and well-being of his community, and especially for the good of underprivileged kids.

He had turned down more than one lucrative offer, refusing to endorse this or that product, for the simple reason that it would counter the model he would have youngsters follow. He turned down an offer to endorse a particular alcoholic beverage, an offer that would have netted him more than a lot of people earn in a whole year, because it would do his image no good. Image was of the essence to Dave Winfield. It was his own image, all right, that meant so much to Dave Winfield; but it was an image, he knew, that meant so much more to others than to himself. It was an image that kids would take as an example for their own lifestyles; it was an image that had gone far beyond what Dave Winfield meant to himself; as Dave saw it, it was an image of exceedingly grave significance to thousands, maybe millions, of kids around the country. It was an image he would guard with all the thought and care he could give it.

In September of 1980 there was doubt in Al Frohman's manner, in his voice: "We have no idea what Dave's market value is. And there's no way we'll know until the draft."

For two years Winfield had managed to avoid the almost complete hitting slump that had plagued him during the second half of every previous season, but in 1980 it returned with a vengeance. At the All-Star break he had been batting .307; by September 10th he had dropped 29 points to .278. He broke out of the slump then; after getting one infield hit in his previous 18 trips, he had a homer and a single against the Giants. It was his 19th homer of the year, his first at the home park since July 24th. He would hit only one more home run the rest of the season.

And then, mercifully, the season was over. Winfield finished with a .276 average, which was 32 points below the previous year's. He had 20 homers and 87 runs batted in, respectable enough for a rookie or the average major-leaguer, but not for a superstar who demanded a million-plus per year, and for five years.

On his final day as a Padre, Dave had a few words for the press. "I know a lot of people think I'll be feeling nostalgic today," he said, "but I won't really. You've got to understand that basically I'm being forced to leave. So no matter what, I couldn't be sentimental about this day. What I had to go through this year I wouldn't wish on anybody. Still, I think I had a decent season. I'm going out with my head up. I'm glad to see this season end."

Gene Tenace had said, "If we lose Winfield, it's like an expansion club again. We've gone backward. Two years ago we won 84 games and finished fourth. Last year we finished in fifth. This year we're in last."

But Winfield could by no means number all the Padres among his admirers. Fireman Rollie Fingers, who was also due to depart and save a lot of games for the Milwaukee Brewers, was openly critical of Dave's attitude.

"Look, Dave has a big ego," he pointed out, "but everybody in this game does. The thing is, you've got to keep it under wraps. He'd come across as if he was better than everybody else on the team. Like he'd say he needed someone hitting behind him, other teams pitched around him, and whatnot. Or that there was no one on the team who could bring out his ability. Well, who wants to hear that bullshit, particularly from a guy who didn't always go to the wall to catch balls, or didn't always dive for the ball? I don't care if the Muppets are batting in front of you, you still got to go out there and put out. Shoot, he'd just come across as better than everybody. He'd go on radio-TV after a game and everything was I-I-me-me. The guys started singing this song, 'Old McWinnie had a farm, me-I-me-I oh.' I sang it myself many times. One of my favorite tunes."

Padres publicity man Bob Chandler blamed Al Frohman for Winfield's woes. He said, "Dave was basically a nice guy, but he had a distorted view of the world from Al Frohman. As an example: There was a banquet in San Diego about two years ago for San Diego's outstanding man. Dave was one of the ten finalists. The guy who eventually won was involved in minority jobs. After the banquet I congratulated Dave for being one of the finalists. He told me, 'What an honor to be in this company. The guy who won deserved it.'

"Then Al Frohman—I actually saw this—went to work on him. Told him, 'What a rotten city. Any other city, Dave Winfield would have won the award.'

"I said to my assistant, Be Barnes, 'You watch. After Al Frohman talks to him, he'll think he got a raw deal.' The next day that's just what Winfield told Be."

Whether it was the pressure of the season or just an off year, Winfield's frequent boast that he could hit better and more consistently with men on base was exploded in 1980. In three major RBI categories he offered practically no competition to such stalwarts as Reggie Jackson and George Brett. For instance:

With runners in scoring position (on second base, third base or both), Winfield batted .224, ranking him 120th in the National League. In the same situation, Jackson hit .301 and Brett a whopping .466.

In the same situation with two out, Dave hit .172. Jackson's figure was .338, Brett's .354.

With two out and a runner on, but not necessarily in scoring position, Winfield hit .216, Jackson .322 and Brett .349.

True, Jackson and Brett were in a different league, but the comparison was valid, because Winfield was slated to become Jackson's teammate, and Brett hit .390 and drove in 118 runs, stamping him as an *authentic* million-dollar player.

But, if the National League had to be the criterion, then there was still Mike Schmidt to be reckoned with. Schmidt had spent much of 1979 chasing Winfield for the RBI title, which Dave eventually won. In 1980 Schmidt was the champion, yet he came to the plate with 50 *fewer* men on base than Winfield.

It was almost anticlimactic when Winfield announced his free agency. Jack McKeon, the new general manager, bravely announced that the loss of Winfield was not crucial, and that the Padres would be about as well off by platooning two other outfielders.

McKeon was absolutely right, Winfield made little difference. At the end of 1981 the Padres were in familiar surroundings—last in the National League West.

12

Just $1.3 Million
a Year

If there had been any hope in San Diego that Dave Winfield would play again for the Padres in 1981, Ray Kroc, the owner of the club, put a virtual end to it with some rather vitriolic remarks in that interview with *Sports Illustrated*.

"I don't want him back," said Ray Kroc, "not even at the price we're paying him now."

The "now" price was $350,000 a year.

"He can't hit with men on base. A dozen times this year he's come up with men on base and hasn't done a damn thing," said Kroc.

"He's afraid of the right field wall, and it's padded," went on the tirade.

The *Sports Illustrated* interviewer asked, "Doesn't Winfield mean a lot to the [San Diego] franchise?"

"He doesn't mean a damn thing," replied Kroc.

The interview took place in the first week of August. For three days, Dave wouldn't say more than a few noncommital sentences on the subject of Kroc's rather devastating remarks on his importance to the ball club and the way he played the game.

"It doesn't pay to dignify those comments with a reply," said Dave, initially. "We've been through enough haggling publicly. I don't want to get into it any more."

Dave, as usual, was leading the Padres in hitting and in runs batted in at the time of the Kroc interview. He was ranked eighth in the League with his RBIs.

It took him a couple of days but he finally took his turn at blasting the owner of the San Diego Padres.

"Naturally," he said, "I didn't appreciate Kroc's comments. He's trying to publicly humiliate me and it isn't going to work. If he doesn't think I'm important to this ball club, then he doesn't know baseball, that's all. The numbers alone show how foolish his comments were."

Whatever Ray Kroc thought of Dave Winfield's value to a ball club, Dave had his own opinion of his worth to a team. And Dave had numbers against which to measure his value, as he saw it.

"Didn't Dave Parker's wife say he was making $1.5 million a year? And didn't the New York Yankees just call in Reggie Jackson and offer him $1.1 million?

"Well, I'm younger, stronger, and better looking than Reggie," said Dave, and he laughed.

He laughed, but he wasn't joking, not about those millions, anyway. Dave Winfield thought and felt very strongly that he belonged up there in the million-dollar brackets.

It was all over now between Dave Winfield and the San Diego Padres, but there were a last few gasping efforts to close the enormous breach that had developed between them. Unfortunately for San Diego—not for Dave Winfield as the situation developed for him—no one involved could say anything of a positive nature. They had cemented themselves into negatives and the negatives continued until Dave's very last days in San Diego.

"If you sign a ballplayer for a lot of years and a lot of money, you expect not only an outstanding performance but a consistent performance," said Ballard Smith. "To a great extent we're being asked to pay Dave Winfield on supposed potential. I feel he has as much potential as anyone in the game. I don't think he's lived up to his potential."

Smith did admit his error in the negotiations for Dave's contract. He allowed that he should not have given the press the proposals that had come from Al Frohman.

Dave's reaction to Smith's remarks was an allover response.

"People," he said, "don't want to get into that right now."

About his value to the San Diego franchise, he said, "It's all a matter of what someone feels you're worth. Take a singer who has tremendous potential. He gets a big offer, let's say. Now does he stay where he is making $10 a week in some hick town, or does he grab the chance to go make $50,000 in Vegas?

"Money isn't the only thing, though," he continued. "Some day people will realize my situation is not all about money, anyway."

Recall that on his last day in San Diego, before his final game for the Padres, Dave had a few words for the press. Those words revealed for the first time some of the deeper emotions he had experienced during his last year in San Diego.

"I know a lot of people think I'll be feeling nostalgic today," he said. "I won't really. You've got to understand that, basically, I'm being forced to leave. So no matter what, I couldn't be sentimental about this day."

It seemed that Dave Winfield was protesting too much, that actually he was more than a bit sentimental about his last day in a Padre uniform, and quite understandably. He had given San Diego eight years, during which time he had grown as a human being and developed into a star ballplayer. Certainly his treatment at the hands of the Padre fans in 1980 may have soured him a bit on San Diego, but there were seven years when he had heard nothing but shouts of approval, as well as great ovations. Dave couldn't forget that if he wanted to.

Still, 1980 was powerful medicine to take.

How about the future? Did Dave Winfield have any anxieties about what lay ahead for him in baseball, in life?

"Not a bit," said Dave, always proud. "I've got a lot of business things planned for the off-season and some vacation time, too. I'm not worried about 1981. In fact, I think I'll probably have a very, very good year."

There was no doubt in Dave's mind about working out a deal with the Dodgers. He had talked with the Dodgers' vice president, Al Campanis, one of the shrewdest of baseball minds. Al had discussed many things with Dave, and it was obvious that Campanis and the Dodgers were greatly interested in further talks. Then too, the Yankees were a strong possibility, and the Kansas City Royals. In any case, as far as Dave was concerned it would have to be a club that could be a challenger for the pennant. And Dave, as might have been expected, wasn't far from seeing his big dream become a reality . . . in 1981.

It was late in October of 1980 when Dave finally cut his ties forever with the San Diego Padres and declared himself a free agent.

13

On the Market

Free agency in 1980 was *not* merely a matter of a baseball player finishing his contract with one team and offering his services to the highest bidder. There were a number of rules and regulations to be followed, but with a few loopholes and escape hatches. True, baseball free agency beginning with 1981 was infinitely more complicated, with enough fine print to keep batteries of bright young attorneys-at-law busy and wealthy explaining the new rules brought about by the compensation agreement, the end result of baseball's midseason strike. But even in 1980 there were occasions when the bosses were not quite certain they were steering the proper course.

When David Winfield cut himself loose from the San Diego Padres, he became a pièce de résistance on the free agent menu. That he should place himself on the sales counter with no ties to anyone was very hard to believe. After all, neither Ballard Smith nor Ray Kroc was stupid. Why would they risk losing Winfield—as they must surely have realized early in the 1980 negotiations—when they could have dealt him away to any of a number of clubs and received something more than a warm body in return? Any number of teams would have been ready to wheel and deal for Winfield, accept his imminent free agency, and take a chance on signing him to a longer contract for a truckload of money. The Dodgers were interested, the Yankees were interested, and the recently purchased New York Mets were right there to dicker with Winfield and Frohman.

To be sure, there was always the possibility that Winfield would play that single year with his new team and still opt for his freedom. That was a consideration tending to drive away all but those of stout heart. Someone like George Steinbrenner, for instance.

It was not a secret that Steinbrenner had his heart set on Winfield. Most of the Yankee power in 1980 had been lefthanded, including Reggie Jackson, Oscar Gamble, and Graig Nettles. The only decent outfielder on the Yankees who swung a bat from the right side of the plate was an aging Lou Piniella, and he could not be considered an everyday regular. Winfield—especially the Winfield of 1978 and 1979— would be a potent addition, and he was the sort of no-nonsense, hustle-type player that Steinbrenner loved.

The Yanks and the Padres had indeed been discussing a trade for Winfield in 1980. Why didn't it go through then? Perhaps for several reasons: maybe the Padres still had some hope of signing Winfield, or maybe they wanted too much in return and Steinbrenner balked at the terms. Perhaps also Al Frohman's initial demands brought a gasp even from the monetarily replete Steinbrenner, who might have hesitated at the thought of submitting to the whims of a player and his agent. For whatever reason, that deal was never consummated.

Following Winfield's sub-par season, Frohman had been forced to trim his sails somewhat. He still wanted a tremendous contract, but such clauses as Frohman's approval before the club could be moved to a new city, or free agency again if the signing team were sold, were immediately discarded. Frohman might have tried bluffing the Padres with such utter nonsense, but heavyweights such as Steinbrenner and O'Malley would have laughed him right out of the business.

Now came the razzle-dazzle legalese of baseball's free agency. Even after Winfield had seemingly severed his ties with San Diego, a trade was still possible. In fact, a trade appeared *mandatory* if Steinbrenner was to acquire Winfield's services.

According to the rules, a maximum of 13 of the 26 major league clubs may draft a free agent, starting with the 13 having the poorest records. The Yankees in 1980 had won 103 games, the best record in baseball. If 13 teams ahead of the Yankees put in their bids for Winfield, Steinbrenner would be shut out, and the mere thought probably struck terror into the breast of Al Frohman.

The same rules permitted a player's old club to continue negotiating with him until three days before the actual draft took place. In fact his old team was the *only team* that could actually discuss the total contract. Other teams could talk to the player or his agent about guarantees or other matters, but money could *not* be mentioned. The draft was scheduled to take place on November 13th; thus the Padres had until November 10th to reach some sort of agreement with Winfield.

If the Padres let him slip away, the only compensation they could expect from the signing team was their pick in the amateur draft (the same kind of draft through which the Padres had secured Winfield in the first place). That wasn't a very attractive prospect, since the Yankees would be drafting 26th and much of the cream of college players would have been taken by then. However, if they signed Winfield, he became their property again and could be traded away at the inter-league winter meetings.

But that, too, was a tricky situation. First of all, the Padres would have to ascertain how much the trading team was willing to allow Winfield to earn. In effect, the Padres would be acting as agents for the Yankees (or some other team), and the Yanks couldn't talk money—with Winfield, that is. Could they talk about money through the Padres? Was that legal according to free-agency rules? That was the second joker in the deck. Nobody would be stupid enough not to realize that Frohman was actually negotiating money with the Yankees, because the Padres had made their position clear repeatedly—they were not about to give Dave Winfield a multiyear, multimillion-dollar contract of the magnitude Frohman demanded.

Using deft sleight of tongue, Marvin Miller, executive director of the

Major League Baseball Players Association (the players' union), declared, "It would require permission from the parties to the basic agreement."

Translated into plainer prose, Miller was saying that such dealings would have to have an agreement first between the Players Association and management's Player Relations Committee.

Miller further expounded, "Our position has been there's nothing wrong with talking terms during this time. A club shouldn't be able to *sign* a player, but there's nothing wrong with using this period for a club and a player to get more information about each other so a club could draft more intelligently. Why shouldn't a potential buyer and seller talk about it before they get to the formal marketplace?"

Ray Grebey, the director of the management committee, wasn't sure about that. He said, "He's declared his free agency and that's another factor. I don't know what the answer is. It hasn't come up before and I haven't thought about it."

Meanwhile, the Yankees and Padres had indeed been talking and there was a deal in the works. The Padres had their eyes on a young Yankee prospect named Joe Lefebvre, who had played briefly with the team before being returned to the minors. Lefebvre had shown some power at the plate and was an excellent fielder with a nice arm.

Jack McKeon, the Padres general manager, said, "The Yankees did ask permission to sign Winfield and we're going to give them permission. But we checked all the procedures and we're not in the inter-league trading period. If we can get a player, major league or minor league, we probably will."

Al Frohman chipped in with what had to be the understatement of the century: "I think David would be willing to talk to the Yankees." Then he added his benediction, "We don't want to hurt the Padres if they can make some sort of trade."

Commissioner Bowie Kuhn, learning of the proposed transaction, offered this gem: "I am aware of it, but I don't normally comment on deals."

While all parties were mulling things over, someone came up with another variation on the theme. Suppose Winfield withdrew his name from the free agent draft and began to negotiate with the Yankees—with the Padres' permission, of course. And suppose further that he failed to come to terms with the Yankees. Could he then resubmit his name for the draft?

Ray Grebey responded, "That's another question we haven't encountered before. I don't know."

Perhaps everybody was too busy contemplating the new problems, or maybe the proposed deal fell through because of its own weight, but for whatever reason, no trade was made. Winfield entered the draft just like any other normal baseball player.

However, the fact that teams like the Yankees or the Dodgers might be shut out because they were at the end of the line was not a pleasant thought for Frohman and Winfield. Accordingly, they dispatched letters to 15 teams, suggesting that it would be a waste of time if they drafted him on the first round because he preferred not to play for them. Winfield gave as his reasons his desire to play for a contending team, and also because he wanted to be in a "metropolitan area" where he could contribute to underprivileged children.

Winfield's intentions may have been honorable, but it certainly appeared that they misdirected a few of the letters. For instance, the mailman made his drop at Baltimore and Pittsburgh; both were "metropolitan centers," both had, sadly, lots of underprivileged kids, and both were usually in the thick of the pennant races. Why didn't Winfield want to play there?

A letter also found its way to Shea Stadium where the Mets held forth. New York is a big city with lots of kids who need things, but the Mets were like blood brothers to the Padres in that they often finished in the cellar.

Bill Veeck, then president of the Chicago White Sox, took a dim view of the letter. "I had intended to draft Dave Winfield," he said. "Not after that letter. Even if he were to sign with us, we don't want him in our town."

Gabe Paul, president of the Celeveland Indians, was similarly exercised when he opened the morning mail. "It's unfair for any player to try to do this," he snapped. "I'm all for allowing every club who wants a player the right to go after him. But this isn't what the owners and other players agreed to, so it's not right for any of us, players or owners, to blatantly try to defeat the principle of the draft."

Al Frohman wasn't too thrilled about the principles of the draft either, but for another reason. As was his custom, he asked and answered his own question.

"What is it, half a draft? When a man becomes a free agent, does he have a right to select the 13 teams he'll talk to? Where is the equity when the owners can select, but the players have nothing to say?"

Gabe Paul regained his equanimity long enough to say that he intended to draft Winfield, regardless of the letter.

Actually, Winfield had not broken new ground with his historic letter. Both Nolan Ryan and Pete Rose had done the same thing when they tossed their names into the hopper, but almost nobody got so excited.

Interestingly, one Yankee who dearly wanted Winfield as his teammate was Reggie Jackson, who said he would do all he could to induce Steinbrenner to sign Dave. Upon hearing this news flash, Calvin Griffith, the owner of the Minnesota Twins, could not resist a hearty chuckle.

"Wouldn't you do the same thing?" he said, referring to Jackson's avowed eagerness. "Reggie has a contract coming up at the end of next season. It would be nice for him to say to Steinbrenner, 'You gave Winfield $1.3 million, now how much are you going to pay me?'"

As D-Day (Draft Day) approached, the name Winfield dominated the sports pages, and the gossip among baseball people centered on the money involved, which, despite all Frohman's and Winfield's denials, was really the bottom line. Pittsburgh manager Chuck Tanner's prediction proved prescient.

"I expect Winfield is going to wind up as the highest-paid player in baseball," he said. "If the New York Yankees are one of the 13 teams to draft him, there's no telling how much money he'll get.

"What I see happening is both the Yankees and the New York Mets drafting Winfield and going after him hard. That would set up a bidding war between them that neither would want to lose. It would also leave Winfield right in the middle, a rather enviable position."

Ten teams drafted Winfield: the New York Mets, the Cardinals, Braves, Pirates, Reds, Astros, Orioles, Angels, Yankees, and Indians.

The Mets, Pirates, Indians, and Orioles had been spurned by Winfield's letters, but they hung in like persistent suitors.

Unhappily for Winfield, the Dodgers did not draft him, although of all the National League teams, they were his first choice. Los Angeles re-signed Dusty Baker, its own star, for a lot less money than they would have had to bid for Winfield.

One by one, for various reasons, drafting teams began to drop out of the bidding. Atlanta's Ted Turner had vowed to remain to the bitter end, but he signed Claudell Washington, a former Met, and was no longer a factor. Gene Autry and his California Angels made only a half-hearted attempt to get him, because Autry had been stung too often with expensive players who failed to produce. In fact, the Angels were the tenth and last team to draft Winfield, and that happened on the fifth round.

Finally the choice was narrowed down to three teams, the Yankees, Mets, and Indians. But the money was still there, so it was not merely a question of who paid how much more than the others. Now, with his future on the line, Winfield had to weigh other considerations, and not necessarily those he had placed on the table before, such as his foundation.

Sign with the Yankees? The team already had a right fielder in Reggie Jackson, the incomparable "Mr. October," a bomber with an ego as big as Winfield's. And there was the ballpark itself to consider. Out in left center a herd of buffalo could graze without crowding—it was that big. "Death Valley," it was called; yet it had been cut down from its previous measurements. Once upon a time, the clouters like Joe DiMaggio and Bill "Moose" Skowron were trying to span the 457 feet to the fence, and it was sad to see grown men cry. Why not, when 450-foot cannon shots were merely loud outs? It wasn't that far now, but far enough. And the Yanks were contenders.

How about the Mets? A possibility. All the team needed was a shortstop who could field, a second baseman who could hit, a first baseman who could play first, a pitching staff, some bench strength, and then they might have a chance to climb out of last place in the National League East. Winfield had just left the counterpart of the Mets on the opposite coast, barely escaping with his sanity.

Ah, but it was New York City, where all the big ad agencies were just panting to part with juicy TV endorsements. It was where all the action was.

Last, and certainly least, there was Cleveland. To paraphrase an old joke, a comic might say, "I spent a week in Cleveland one day." It was a club constantly rebuilding, but somehow the contractors never managed to rise above the first floor.

But there was a prospective owner named James Nederlander and a California lawyer named Neil Papiano, and they began mentioning a career in the entertainment industry when Winfield's playing days were done.

Then suddenly Winfield signed with Steinbrenner's Yankees.

George Mitchell Steinbrenner III, principal owner of the New York Yankees, has been described in any number of ways. Charitable: when Elston Howard, the first black Yankee and an outstanding baseball player, passed away, Steinbrenner quietly took care of the medical bills. It was some time before anyone found out who had paid all the doctor and hospital bills.

A martinet, difficult to work for: he has fired and rehired his employees so often that few take him seriously when he dismisses them. He hired Billy Martin to manage the Yankees, fired him and replaced Martin with Bob Lemon. Then he replaced Lemon with Billy Martin (while still paying Lemon). Martin was canned once more and replaced by Dick Howser. Howser was out and in came Gene Michaels. Michaels was fired and back came Bob Lemon. Last anyone heard, Michaels was due back at the helm in 1983.

Any questions?

A dedicated American: well, why not? Like George M. Cohan and Yankee Doodle Dandy, Steinbrenner was born on the Fourth of July (1930).

A man who loves kids: Steinbrenner once paid all the bills for a weekend in New York for a Cleveland high school basketball team, and the only reason he gave was, "Nobody ever does anything for the good kids." With Steinbrenner, funding scholarships is almost a reflex action. He has paid the tuition for more than 60 scholar athletes, referred to him

by friends, who knew George would handle everything and without any
fanfare.

An admirer of all things military: probably the result of attending
Culver Military Academy in Indiana, starting at age thirteen. His friend,
Bill Fugazy, who runs a limousine service in New York, once remarked,
"He's the only guy I know who walks around humming the theme from
Patton."

A lover of sports: at Culver, Steinbrenner played football (end) and
ran track (hurdles). He ran the hurdles at Williams College, too, and was
a rough and tough competitor.

A cultured man: Steinbrenner is devoted to the classics, with a special
fondness for Shakespeare. He was also president of his college glee club
and dabbled at writing a sports column for the Williams *Record.*

A self-made millionaire: and thereby hangs the tale.

George Steinbrenner was born into an affluent family and grew up in
Bay Village, a suburb of Cleveland. Henry Steinbrenner, his father, was a
graduate of Massachusetts Institute of Technology. The Steinbrenner
income was derived from a company called Kinsman Marine Transit, a
Great Lakes shipping company, the family business since the 1840s.

Steinbrenner, Senior, did not believe in coddling his children. Instead
of giving his son an allowance, he bought George some chickens and
ordered him to make his own money by selling the eggs. Even then
George knew how to turn a buck. He called his operation the George
Company and made a tidy profit, until he had to sell his assets to his
sisters because he was leaving for Culver.

After Williams College, George was a first lieutenant in the U.S.A.F.
Strategic Air Command from 1952 to 1954. When mustered out he
should have gone home to the family business, but he never could resist
the blandishments of sports. In Columbus he coached high school
football and basketball; then, in 1955, he became an assistant coach for
Lou Saban, who was head coach at Northwestern University. In 1956 he
moved on to Purdue, where he was the backfield coach. Saban is now a
Yankee vice president.

George Steinbrenner is very wealthy now, but he wasn't then. Not
only was his salary small, but Kinsman Transit wasn't doing well either,

and he had to help bail out the company. For three years father and son scrounged for business, and finally landed a big contract to ship Jones & Laughlin steel. That was back somewhere around 1960; George was thirty years old and practically starting from scratch.

Steinbrenner experienced some setbacks himself. With borrowed money he organized a group of people who backed an industrial league basketball team, the Cleveland Pipers. It was a championship team, but pro basketball was rising and the league folded. Often George had to make the rounds in order to scrape up enough to cover the team's payroll.

So it was back to the drawing board, and Steinbrenner threw in his lot with a group that purchased the American Ship Building Company, with shipyards in Tampa, Cleveland, and other cities. It was then that the Steinbrenner touch asserted itself and his fortunes escalated.

Sports, however, were as much a part of George Steinbrenner as his breathing apparatus and bloodstream. He wanted to own a team, and what Steinbrenner wants, Steinbrenner gets—well, most of the time. Baseball had not, in the past, been his *forte,* although while in the Air Force he managed a team that did fairly well. He told *New York Daily News* writer Mike Lupica, "I used to have a book about baseball. I knew nothing about it, but I used to stay one chapter ahead of the guys, and that's the way I coached."

Lack of knowledge notwithstanding, Steinbrenner made an offer to buy the Cleveland Indians, but the owner of the club, Vernon Stouffer, was in no tearing hurry to make a decision. While Steinbrenner was waiting, he heard that CBS was willing to unload the Yankees at a loss. Steinbrenner waited no longer.

Back in 1925, Tim Mara, a wealthy "sportsman" (a nice way to say gambler in those days), bought a franchise from the National Football League, put together a team—and thus was founded the New York Giants. Mara paid $500 for the franchise, and *that* was the greatest sports bargain of all time.

George Steinbrenner didn't do too badly, either. On January 3, 1973, Steinbrenner headed a syndicate which purchased the Yankees from the Columbia Broadcasting System for $10 million. It is also interesting to note that in 1946 a group headed by Dan Topping bought the Yankees for about $3 million, while CBS later paid $13 million. Those who enjoy toying with higher mathematics can better understand the magnitude of Winfield's deal, which called for much more than $20 million—over twice as much as Steinbrenner's bunch paid for the *entire team,* lock, stock and barrel. But that was okay too, because in 1980 the Yankees showed a net profit of $7.5 million.

It could, in a way, be said that Steinbrenner and his people bought damaged goods, because the once-proud image of the New York Yankees was badly tarnished when he took over. In 1964 CBS had purchased the team and turned over its stewardship to a personable and heroic gentleman (he had been an O.S.S. officer in World War II) named Michael Burke. That was the same year the Yankees won the American League pennant. Long twilight years followed, years which saw the team flounder helplessly. In 1966, for example, the team finished tenth and last.

Supposedly loyal fans deserted the Yankees; one game drew a "crowd" of 413 paid admissions. CBS wanted to get out from under and looked around for a buyer, but none could be found until Steinbrenner surfaced. Burke was a member of Steinbrenner's syndicate that bought the club, and he still owns a share. Steinbrenner became the principal owner.

It was George Steinbrenner who turned the team around, Steinbrenner and no one else. Although he had indicated he wouldn't interfere much with the day-to-day operations of the Yankees, he just couldn't help himself. The Yankees of today are his handiwork. But, before he could get down to serious work on the team, first he had to get rid of a huge political albatross that threatened to destroy him. Part of the story came out in the Watergate hearings.

Although never a "clubhouse Democrat," that was nevertheless the party of his choice. He was instrumental in helping to raise large sums of money for congressional candidates, and numbered among his friends such political notables as Ted Kennedy and Tip O'Neill. According to some sources, Richard Nixon's people saw a financial threat in Steinbrenner and set out to stop him, partly through an antitrust investigation of American Ship Building. There were to be Internal Revenue Service audits and perhaps even the loss of important port licenses.

Rather than endure a protracted legal session, Steinbrenner tried to use the political elixir that had always worked for others in the past—money. He made a personal contribution of $75,000 to CREEP—the Committee to Re-Elect the President—and also gave eight of his executives "bonuses" of $25,000 each, which were also to be given to the committee, a grand total of $275,000.

Rumor had it that the Nixon forces were still not satisfied. They squeezed harder, demanding information George might have discovered concerning various influential Democrats, and there Steinbrenner drew the line. When he wouldn't come across, he was indicted on fourteen counts of alleged conspiracy to violate the campaign funding laws. Actually, Steinbrenner had been forced to contribute to the CREEP fund, which in itself was illegal but par for the course in politics.

Steinbrenner pleaded guilty to two of the charges. His friends say he took the rap rather than rock the boat. He was fined $15,000, and Kuhn suspended him from baseball for the entire 1975 season.

Also not of his making was free agency, the rule that turned utility infielders into readers of the Dow Jones stock market averages. The Yankees were accused of paying mind-blowing salaries to the newly emancipated players, but so did the California Angels, the Houston Astros, the Philadelphia Phillies—yes, the San Diego Padres, too. The difference was, Steinbrenner seldom made a mistake.

Other clubs tried to deal for Catfish Hunter, but Steinbrenner got him. Reggie Jackson was declared a free agent, but he signed with the Yankees. Ron Guidry might have elected to leave New York when his contract was up, but he re-signed with New York. True, Don Gullett developed arm miseries and wasn't much use, but everybody's entitled to one miscalculation.

Having paid his money, Steinbrenner has always expected to get full value, and those who dog it on the field are called "$100,000 bums." He is, in a sense, the Vince Lombardi of baseball, to whom losing a game is a mortal sin.

"I want failure to be so distasteful to my players that they hate to lose or to make a mistake," he said. He has castigated his players publicly for throwing to the wrong base, for ill-advised base running, for missing a sign, and for lack of hustle. He is equally quick with the kudos. The circus catches executed by Graig Nettles in the 1978 World Series left him practically speechless.

"Super! Nettles was absolutely super," was all he could say.

This, then, was the man with whom Dave Winfield cast his lot. Later, during spring training, Winfield remarked, "I read more about Steinbrenner than I know from experience."

On December 15, 1980, at a jam-packed news conference at Jimmy Weston's cafe, on New York's smart East Side, with Yankees Reggie Jackson, Willie Randolph, Rick Cerone, and manager Gene Michael, among others, in attendance, George Steinbrenner introduced Dave Winfield as the newest player to wear the pinstriped Yankee uniform.

George had won the battle for the services of Dave Winfield. Dave had won the battle for the values he had put on his services to play ball.

It was an incredible contract the big kid out of St. Paul signed. It called for ten years at a minimum of $1.3 million for the first year, plus a bonus of $1 million for signing the contract. The contract calls for 10 years with a 10 percent cost of living bonus each year. Thus with the cost-of-living proviso, Dave could receive $3.5 million in the tenth year, when he will be 39. Additional bonus money will amount to a total deal of more than $23,000,000.

They began to call Dave the 23 million dollar man, and that didn't make Dave feel bad at all. There were only a half dozen or so others in baseball who pulled down anywhere near that kind of money in 1981. They were a very select group of players: Nolan Ryan of the Astros, Phil Niekro of the Braves, Andre Dawson of the Expos, George Brett of the Royals, and Dave Parker of the Pirates.

Dave didn't quite take this sudden good fortune in his usual easy stride. It shocked him a bit. He had to get used to it.

"Funny," he said. "I'm the same person I've been for a long, long time, and it's only in these past couple of months that I've gotten any real recognition. I guess it's the New York newspapers, magazines, television that made the difference. I'm the same ballplayer I was last year, and the year before, and now, all at once, I'm a household name. They're writing and talking about me everywhere. Even Johnny Carson is talking about me. I don't comprehend it fully. I'm just going along with the flow."

It was a beautiful flow and Dave Winfield enjoyed every minute of his new journey into fame.

Curiously enough, or consistently enough, Dave insisted that money was far from the most important consideration in his contractual negotiations. Nor was it the money George Steinbrenner offered him that finally had him sign up with the Yankees. According to Al Frohman, backing up Dave's contention, Dave had been offered substantially more money, almost unbelievably more money, by other clubs.

The money did have importance for Dave, and he said so. But there were other factors of equal and perhaps greater importance for the ballplayer.

There was his Winfield Foundation.

"Fifty-five percent of the mail on the Foundation comes from the New York area," he said. "The potential growth of the Foundation is very important for me."

Playing for a winning team, as he had indicated so often, was also important for Dave.

"I always played with a winning team," he said, "before I played for the Padres.

"The Yankees are winners," he said. "George Steinbrenner is a winner.

"You play for a losing club," added Dave, "and you get to be known as a loser, no matter how well you play the game, no matter what you do with your bat."

That bat was important for Dave, too.

"With the Padres," he said, "I never got a good pitch to hit. I was surprised when I got a good pitch. With the San Diego Padres, pitchers could pitch all around me. It didn't cost them anything to put me on base, not with the lineup behind me."

Joe Torre, back in 1979, had ordered his pitcher to put Dave on first base once, with the bases loaded and two men out, according to Dave. And Tom Lasorda fined his pitchers if they gave Dave anything to hit with a man on base.

"They'll have to pitch to me on the Yankees," said Dave, "with men like Jackson and Piniella and Cerone and Nettles, and all the rest of them in the lineup."

It may have been that, for all his self-confidence, Dave was not really sure of how good a ballplayer he was, and that he wanted to find out.

"I never hit in a lineup with some decent players," he said. "When you're the top dog, you get ulcers and heart attacks. I've had enough ulcers. I'm better off with players who play as well as I do, or even better. That makes me better."

In December 1980 that was a moot question. He was the 23 million dollar man, but would he be worth it to the Yankees? Would he really show the great abilities he believed he had? Would that universally recognized potential of his finally blossom with the Yankees and Dave emerge as the best of them all with the New York club?

There were all-time greats in the history of the Yankees: Babe Ruth, Lou Gehrig, Joe DiMaggio, and Mickey Mantle, among others. Was Dave Winfield to join that celebrated list of baseball immortals? The potential was there. Would it be realized? Time, and only time, would tell.

14

The 23 Million Dollar Man

While the Winfield multimillion contract did not result in a storm of controversy, nevertheless there were many who ridiculed the idea of paying all that money to a lifetime .284 batter. Some pointed to Pete Rose—"Charlie Hustle"—whose contract with the Philadelphia Phillies called for much less on a per annum basis. Giving Rose a lot of money was understandable. He had produced any number of better than 200-hit seasons, he was colorful, he drew crowds; and he always gave them their money's worth with his headlong dives into a base. Rose was, in effect, an All-Star utility man who could play the outfield, third base or first base. But what had Dave Winfield done to become King of the Hill?

Even before Winfield signed with the Yankees, catcher Rick Cerone had some misgivings about the end result of acquiring the big outfielder.

"It's the front office's job to determine what we need, not mine," Cerone said. "But everybody should see the one thing we need most is a righthanded starter. It's going to be awfully hard to repeat as American League East champs without one."

Cerone was not necessarily envious of the millions being bandied about in order to lure Winfield; he merely doubted that one player could make the Yankees world champions.

"I don't agree with the theory that one player makes a team," Cerone argued. "I look in our division and see a lot of guys who had good years with bad teams. If we get Winfield and he has a good year but a lot of guys on the team don't, we'll still finish third or fourth. This game is based upon a total team effort. One player won't make the difference."

Winfield himself would have been the first to agree with Cerone. He had hit 154 home runs during his career with the Padres, 78 in the last three seasons, but San Diego never went anywhere. In fact they never finished as high as third.

Cerone also foresaw a potential problem positioning Winfield. Reggie Jackson was the right fielder; Winfield had always boasted that he was the best right fielder in baseball. Jackson was an indifferent fielder, but his bat was necessary. The October Man was too valuable to be relegated to designated-hitter duties.

"I hit 40 home runs last year, and I'm sure they'll find a spot for me. I'm sure they'll find spots for both of us," Jackson said sagely.

Jackson had also remarked, "If we got Winfield and we lost, maybe George would blame him and not just me."

Winfield also received a piece of advice from Jackson regarding how to deal with New York's fans and the Big Apple's media. Supposedly they were sophisticated, not like the small town people (comparatively) of San Diego and St. Paul.

"The bottom line is that if Dave Winfield hits and drives in runs, it doesn't matter if he does or doesn't talk," said elder statesman Jackson. "If you hit the ball over the wall, everything else takes care of itself. My advice to him is to play like hell and put numbers on the board."

And, of course, both media and fans were beginning to question the million-dollar salaries of ball players. One California fan, commenting on pitcher Don Sutton's new three-year, three-million-dollar pact with the Houston Astros, thought that America was on its way down as a great power:

"How can any society place such a grotesque, outlandish value on sports participants? I enjoy watching baseball and football games, but when I think of how much money these athletes are pulling in, it makes me sick. The Russians will never have to take over our society by force. We will cease to exist, as the Roman Empire evaporated."

As for the "pressure" felt by Winfield or others in having to justify those big numbers, a California grounds crew employee observed succinctly, "Reggie Smith, he say pressure is trying to feed eight kids and a wife on $90 a week with the rent due."

Yet Winfield had indeed placed his career—his professional life—on the chopping block. In the past he had grumbled about being the only big fish in a small pond, a complaint echoed frequently by Al Frohman.

"Dave was naked in the Padres lineup," Frohman said stoutly. "He had eight years of frustration. He wants a chance to play with a team of talent, a team like the New York Yankees."

Then he added some words which he might have wished later that he had not uttered:

"He wants a chance to play in a World Series so he can show the country just how good a player Dave Winfield is."

Truly, Dave Winfield was no longer naked. He was now clothed in a lineup with good batters standing ahead of and behind him. He was now literally surrounded by the likes of All-Star second baseman Willie Randolph, former Padres teammate Jerry Mumphrey (acquired by Steinbrenner in a trade), power hitters such as Jackson, Gamble, Graig Nettles, steady contact hitters with years of experience such as Bob Watson, Bucky Dent, and Lou Piniella. Nor could he cast aspersions on the pitching staff, not with such proven winners as Tommy John, Ron Guidry, Rudi May and young Dave Righetti, plus overwhelming strength in the bullpen, which could call on Ron Davis and the incomparable Goose Gossage to put out incipient fires.

Ballard Smith, Winfield's old adversary, said it all on the eve of the 1981 season: "For Dave Winfield, there are no more excuses now."

Winfield knew the score and realized he was being scrutinized with the intensity of a lab researcher staring at bacteria. All he really needed was an opportunity to get rolling and not be judged too hastily. Most of the superstar free agents signed by the Yankees in the past had started off poorly. Catfish Hunter, the first of Steinbrenner's millionaires, lost his first three games. In his first four starts he went 0-3 with a 7.27 earned run average. Reggie Jackson was hitting .194 after his first eight games. The vaunted Goose Gossage gave up three home runs in his first four appearances and didn't save a game throughout the month of April.

Even Cerone, although he had hoped for a righty pitcher, understood what a hazing Winfield might have to endure if he sputtered at the plate.

"I read in the papers how much Dave is getting," Cerone said, "and they say he'd better hit homers for that. Someone else said that because Dave is being paid three times as much as Reggie, he'd better hit three times as well. That's impossible. How's he supposed to hit 120 homers?"

At spring training in Fort Lauderdale, Winfield had an early indication of what might be in store. For some reason—perhaps the dust or hay fever—Dave had a sneezing attack. Then he stepped into the batting cage to face Tommy John, whose curve and screwball had fooled Winfield when both were in the National League. He swung at 10 pitches, fouling off four of them.

"One more swing," Winfield begged, and hit a soft fly to the outfield.

He went back into the cage later for another stint, this time against a young pitcher trying to show his stuff. Winfield fouled off 9 of 13 swings. It was obvious that his swing wasn't grooved and his timing was off. But it was, after all, his first attempt to swing a bat since his farewell game as a Padre.

Throughout the spring training season and into the exhibition games, Winfield was too eager, too tense, and did poorly. He struck out some, popped up, grounded out, and got an occasional base hit. And he had to keep answering the same questions submitted to him by different sportswriters from various newspapers.

No, he didn't expect any problems with Reggie Jackson, they were both professionals, playing for the same team. And no, he didn't want to classify himself as a home-run hitter. He was a line-drive hitter, much more interested in base hits and runs batted in. Yes, he felt the pressure and was doing his best to cope with it.

Winfield was being most circumspect in his responses. Jackson, in his first season as a Yankee, had sounded off a bit too exuberantly when interviewed by a sports magazine.

"I," he said, with his ego showing, "am the straw that stirs the drink."

Jackson's humor did not set well with the late Thurman Munson, the captain of the Yankees. Munson was the team leader, not merely self-proclaimed but looked up to by the rest of the Yankees. He was not about to permit this rank outsider to usurp his position. Jackson later apologized for his flippant remark and outwardly the feud cooled, but Munson never really forgave him.

Winfield continued to lunge for pitches and once again it was a batting coach who picked up the flaw in his mechanics. Previously, Bob Skinner and others had pointed out the hitch in Dave's swing; now it was Charley Lau who took him in hand. It was Lau who had worked with George Brett while at Kansas City and helped make him one of the deadliest batters in either league.

This time it was relatively simple. Winfield was standing too close to the plate, and inside pitches handcuffed him. Lau suggested that Winfield back off somewhat. From that position in the batter's box, with his long arms, he could still reach out and go to right field with an outside pitch. With his line drive power he could probably reach the short fence.

Although the Yankees had seen dismal days while Mike Burke was running the team, one thing he did succeed in doing was to coax New York City into refurbishing Yankee Stadium. Originally budgeted at $24 million, the cost had somehow escalated to $100 million; and it was difficult to pin down the exact cause. However, all that was temporarily forgotten on opening day, 1981. A crowd of 55,123 patrons filed through the turnstiles, plus 250 more from the media in the press facilities, the largest opening-day mob since the stadium reopened in 1976. They had come not only to watch a baseball game but to get a look at the 23 million dollar man in the performance of his duty.

So far, during the Grapefruit League exhibition games, Winfield had been a distinct disappointment. In 85 times at bat he had hit a meager .212, with no home runs, only nine runs batted in and he'd struck out ten times. Now he was like a much-heralded rookie wheeled out for display. A number of the fans were openly skeptical of Winfield's supposed talents:

"I heard he doesn't hit that good."

"They could've gotten two players for the price of one, Sutton for $3.5 million and Fred Lynn for $3 million."

"He's a Yankee so I'll cheer for him, but I want him to prove he's worth the money."

Winfield's best friend on the team, Bob Watson, offered the usual advice, but it was really up to Dave. "I told him to relax and play his own game, but your mental side is one thing and your human side is another," Watson shrugged.

The Texas Rangers had faced the Yankees five times during the exhibition season and had seen Winfield swing at almost anything. He had been tense, excited, and overanxious in Florida and there was no reason to suppose he'd do anything differently, especially with opening-day butterflies cavorting through his insides.

In his first turn at bat, Winfield walked on five pitches.

Ruefully, Texas catcher Jim Sundberg later confessed, "Today we had to throw him strikes. He was much more selective than in Florida."

Bob Watson then banged what looked like a routine double-play grounder. Winfield took off for second with that easy loping gait—"nine strides and a slide" was the way he described it—and when he hit the dirt his skidding, driving hook slide took Ranger shortstop Mario Mendoza out of the play, preventing him from relaying the ball to first. The crowd gave him a hand for that.

Winfield came up again in the third and lofted out to center, but in the fifth, with lefty Jon Matlack on the mound, Winfield swung at a jamming pitch on his fists and popped one to right for a single. It was his first hit as a Yankee that really counted. Watson followed with a hit through the middle and Winfield tore around second and went to third easily. Watching him, sportscaster Tony Kubek, once a marvelous Yankee shortstop, commented admiringly on the way Winfield did things.

"You get to the Hall of Fame on hitting and pitching," Kubek said. "Those statistics are variable. But it's the constants that win games. It's running without using a coach, fielding, throwing. Those are the constants, and Winfield's great at constants. Sometimes he'll take an extra out away from the other team with his fielding, by holding a man to a single thereby setting up a double play, and sometimes he'll give the Yankees an extra out by taking second with that quick start out of the batter's box. He's worth every penny he gets."

In the seventh inning Winfield's base hit started a five-run surge that won the game. In the eighth inning the patient Winfield hung in while relief pitcher Charlie Hough rode the count to 3-and-2 on him, then he calmly took ball four. Altogether his 2-for-3 game with a pair of walks was totally satisfying, especially since the Yanks won, 10-3.

Winfield's opening day play received excellent notices from both the press and the fans, and Winfield's elation was evident in what he said and the way he said it: "The fans here are terrific. They live and breathe baseball. . . . I'm willing to work hard and pay my dues . . . everything is ahead. There'll be good days and bad days, but mostly good."

Sometimes Winfield mixed the good and the bad, as in a 5-1 victory to which he contributed. He got one hit and was robbed of another by a fine fielding play. And he stole second with a head-first slide. But manager Gene Michael wasn't too thrilled with the steal, because he ran on his own, with slugger Oscar Gamble coming up.

It was not until April 29th that Winfield managed to reach the seats with one of his drives. It was a game to remember on all counts, because Dave was the real story behind the win over the Tigers.

The Yankees trailed 1-0 when they came to bat in the top of the third. With one out, Bucky Dent doubled and Jerry Mumphrey singled him home knotting the score. Winfield dug in against starter Jack Morris, and he promptly lashed a line drive just over the fence in right field to give the Yanks a 3-1 lead.

"Too bad it wasn't a home run I could stand and watch," Winfield grinned after the game, "so I could show the guys my trot." It was a good-natured dig at Reggie; when he hit one out he knew it, the pitcher knew it, and the fans knew it, because it was gone the moment it left the bat, gone in a cloud-skimming arc. Reggie would stand at the plate momentarily, watching the ball fade into the sea of shirt sleeves, then go into his patented home run gait.

As Winfield rounded first he pointed a finger at his mates on the bench as if to say, "I did it, didn't I?" When he returned to the dugout, high-fiving everyone in sight, the Yankees gave him the full treatment. In the past, when a light hitter like Fred "Chicken" Stanley hit a rare home run, he would return to the bench and find Jackson on the floor feigning a dead faint. For Winfield, it was Aurelio Rodriguez lying prone, eyes closed.

Someone else remarked, "Derrel Thomas also has one home run this season, and he's six inches shorter and 60 pounds lighter than you."

Winfield took the ribbing gladly. To him it was a sign that he belonged, he was accepted, he was pulling his weight but not carrying the team on his back. The fact that his homer proved to be the game-winner was another source of satisfaction.

"If I was in San Diego," he said, "I'd be hearing, 'You're hitting over .300, but you've only got one home run and nine RBIs, and you're batting cleanup. You're not doing your job.' That's the difference in New York. We've got nine professional dudes out there."

Winfield's bat was only part of his contribution to that win. He carried a potent glove, one capable of taking runs away from the opposition. In the fifth inning the Tigers got two runners on with nobody out. Lou Whitaker, trying to sacrifice them along, fouled off two pitches, then popped a Texas leaguer into short left. Winfield had been playing shallow, but he had a long way to go. At the last minute he lunged forward, slid along his belly and grabbed the ball.

Reggie Jackson praised his new teammate to the skies. "He plays the whole game and he wants to play, he likes to play. He's always saying to me, 'C'mon, big guy, let's go, me and you.' I expected him to be one helluva player, and so far I haven't seen anything I didn't expect. And he's going to get better once he learns the umpires and the cities and the fans, and the coaches and managers learn about him."

Those other managers Jackson mentioned tried hard to throw Winfield off stride, but he had his own brand of rebuttal. Billy Martin, field boss of the Oakland Athletics, a baseball man who tried every angle, attempted to disparage Winfield, saying, "He's the softest hitter I ever saw for a guy who's six-six."

Winfield chuckled, "Billy's style is to antagonize and intimidate, but he can't do that to me because, first, I don't work for him; second, I'm not a marshmallow salesman; and three, if he needs a loan, tell him to call me for an appointment."

One time, with Dave at the plate, Martin climbed to the top step of the dugout and dramatically waved his outfielders to come in shallow. Winfield gleefully responded by crashing a double off the 430-foot marker.

"I never saw a line drive hit harder," said Gene Michael.

Martin ate his words gracefully: "That drive would have been a home run in the National League."

There was something strange about Winfield's attitude during the first part of the 1981 season. With the Padres, he had practically carried the attack single-handed; going into June, he was performing somewhat the same chore for the Yankees, but nary a complaint escaped his lips. Experienced hitters such as Piniella, Gamble, and Jackson were mired in deep slumps (Jackson was batting .199) but Winfield picked up the slack. After the first 31 games of the season, Dave was the leading Yankee hitter with a .345 average, and he kept on hitting, as in the game against Kansas City, with the Royals up by 5-1 in the third. With two on, Winfield drilled one into the stands to make the score 5-4. One out later, Graig Nettles clubbed another homer to tie the score. The Yanks went on to win, 8-5.

By June 10th Winfield had almost nothing left to prove as far as the American League was concerned. He was batting .328, eighth highest in the American League. He led the Yankees in hits with 67, in doubles with 13, and in runs batted in with 40. Despite denials that he was a home-run hitter, he was tied for the club lead with seven homers, and had scored 32 runs, only one less than leadoff batter Willie Randolph.

Always regarded as an outstanding ball-hawk, now his fielding was a revelation. He had played every game so far, 14 of them in center field when Mumphrey was sidelined, and had not made an error. Nobody took liberties with his arm. He had always boasted that he was the best right fielder in baseball; he should have amended that to say he was one of the finest all-around outfielders in the game.

"Winfield is the most valuable Yankee," Jackson declared. "He's been great. We had lunch today for two hours. He was more or less telling me, 'Keep rolling, buddy.'"

Someone asked, "Was he giving you advice?"

"I'd call it support," Reggie smiled. "He's a good guy, I very much appreciate that."

In the middle of June, Winfield's heroics came to an abrupt pause, but it was not of his doing. For months there had been talk of a baseball strike over compensation when a team signed a free agent. The owners had been demanding more than a selection from the amateur draft from the team signing one of their lost stars; they wanted a front line player as well. They proposed that each team protect 15 to 18 players, with the rest subject to loss.

The players were more or less in agreement with the basic idea of a team losing a good player when it drafted a star, but they disagreed as to the number of good players subject to loss. They also objected to the pre-draft free-agent draft the owners wanted.

At the time preliminary discussions had been held, the owners had the right to put their proposed plan into operation by June 1, 1981. The baseball players had the right to strike the same day.

June 1st went by; nothing happened. But a strike seemed inevitable anyway. The National Labor Relations Board got into the act, requesting an injunction on the proposed action by the owners, claiming that the owners had bargained in bad faith. U.S. District Court Judge Henry Werker denied the injunction. That was the first week in July.

"If there's a strike, the card game is in my room," Winfield proclaimed.

The players put on a brave front, trying to pretend that a strike wasn't the worst thing that could happen. The fans were ambivalent. Some thought the strike would happen, others thought it wouldn't.

"Those guys make too much dough," one fan was quoted. "They're not going to give up any of it."

Others felt a strike was imminent. For almost a century ball players had been virtually chattels of the club owners and at last had been emancipated through free agency. To give in now might well begin a process of erosion of power which could, down the road, lead to even further weakening of the Players Association.

Winfield was solidarity personified. "Like everybody else I hope there won't be a strike," he said. "But if there is, you can be sure I'll go out like everybody else. I stick with the whole group. If it hadn't been for the group, for Marvin Miller and the Players Association, I wouldn't be where I am today. None of us would be."

Someone called Dave's attention to the money he would be losing. Dave reflected on that, thinking of his mother, who had a very decent job with the St. Paul Board of Education.

"It's funny," he shook his head, "I was figuring the other day, if we're out on strike for only two weeks, I would lose as much money as my mother would make in four and a half or five years on her job."

On the morning of June 12th, Marvin Miller, executive director of the Players Association, announced the end, if only temporarily, of the baseball season. The strike was on.

After the initial shock of summer without baseball had worn off, the fans began to grumble. They were glowering primarily at the players, and in one sense no one could really blame them. It was hard for John Doe of Middle-Class America to sympathize with someone whose take-home pay was ten, twenty, or fifty times his own. They saw utility players, mediocrities batting .235, earning $100,000–$150,000 a year, and shook their heads in disbelief.

Rusty Staub, the player representative for the New York Mets, tried to explain his colleagues' cause. "When sanitation men go on strike, people get mad," he said. "When there's no baseball, I guess the fans will get mad. I only hope they understand that we never wanted this."

Staub's analogy was not well taken. There was, after all, a world of difference between a sanitation strike and a walkout by baseball players. One might lead to an epidemic with rats infesting the city streets, the other merely to the loss of an afternoon's or evening's entertainment. Besides, how many sanitation workers were pulling down $100,000 a year for six months' work?

It was true that club owners were making money with their franchises, but they claimed the profit margin was dwindling. Ray Kroc had constantly complained that he was losing money with the Padres. That may or may not have been so; creative arithmetic is not unknown in sports. Ruly Carpenter, whose family had owned the Philadelphia Phillies for years, finally threw in the towel and sold out for $30 million. Carpenter never pleaded poverty, but he saw the inflated salaries as sheer madness which would eventually kill baseball.

After some seven weeks of bargaining, a complicated agreement was reached. It involved "Type A" and "Type B" players, based on the statistics of their two most recent seasons. Each club was permitted to protect a certain number of players, 24 if they signed someone considered a ranking free agent, 26 if they signed a nonranking player. All unprotected players were placed in a "compensation pool."

A team losing a "Type A" (ranking) player would be permitted to select a player from the pool (even if that player did not belong to the team that signed a star through free agency), plus the signing team's first amateur draft choice. Loss of a "Type B" player allowed the losing team to select the signing team's first-round amateur draft choice plus a special second choice following the first round of the June draft. A team losing an unranked player who had been selected by four or more teams received only a draft choice. If fewer than four teams selected an unranked player, no compensation was necessary.

There was a limit to the number of free agents who would qualify for payment from the compensation pool, that number depending on the number of clubs in the pool, ranging from seven to eight the first year, nine in the second and third years.

A club losing a player from the compensation pool would be paid $150,000, the money coming from a central fund established by the 26 teams of both leagues.

The players also demanded and got full service credit for the time lost while they were on strike. Service credit was important, for it determined eligibility for future free agency, salary arbitration, and pension time.

Winfield, meanwhile, had not been idle. As the first signs of a breakthrough in the strike appeared, with the knowledge that an All-Star game would be played after all, Dave rushed through plans for his annual kids' party. The whole thing was arranged in less than two weeks by Dave, his brother, Steve, Al Frohman, and Debbie McIntosh, the Community Coordinator of the Foundation. A lot of other people came forward to help with their time, their efforts, and their merchandise.

"It was quite a roundup," Debbie smiled tiredly. "We got the kids from New York and from New Jersey. We got them through the Board of Education, the YMCA, the PAL, the Boy Scouts and the Girl Scouts."

About 13,000 kids had been invited, with the expectation that 11,000 would show up. The actual count was closer to 20,000. They came to gawk at Dave, and at Bucky Dent, Bob Watson, Jerry Mumphrey, Ron Davis, and others.

There were medical exams; about 300 kids were put through the routine—it would have taken a week to look at all of them. But everybody got autographs and a bag lunch consisting of juice, milk, cheese, ice cream, and vitamins. There were T-shirts, and 25 kids got new shoes. Then on to the baseball clinic at Randall's Island Park where the event was staged. The Harlem Wizard's, a professional basketball group, showed up to go through their clowning basketball antics. All in all it was a typical Winfield party.

"Playing the Baltimore Orioles is easier than this," sighed the bone-weary Winfield. "But I wouldn't have missed it for anything."

So the great baseball strike of 1981 was history, but the memory would linger for a long time. Some of the players, such as Rusty Staub, could not conceal a touch of bitterness.

"I am very pleased we have a settlement," he said, "but it was a destructive thing to our game, to the business of baseball. And their [the owners'] all-out attack was to get exactly what they wanted or to break the Players Association. I am very displeased about that." Staub then added, "We went 50 days into a situation which never should have gone into a strike."

Steve Rogers, the Montreal Expos pitcher, echoed Staub's sentiments. "Any time you stand toe to toe with illogical viewpoints and you try to use logic, there will be frustration. And frustration breeds bitterness. You leave with something of a sour taste in your mouth. We're only human. This is not something you come away from feeling ecstatic."

Jim Palmer, Baltimore's veteran pitcher, felt the same way. "I guess I'm just saddened that this couldn't have been circumvented," he said. "Maybe baseball can learn something and come up with a better way to resolve differences."

Gene Michael, the Yankee field skipper, was really part of management, but he also had to live with his players, and therefore his remarks were extremely tactful.

"I just got tired of answering questions," he said. "Otherwise, I held up pretty well. I played a lot of golf, but I didn't get any better at it."

Yankee second baseman Willie Randolph looked at the strike and the settlement this way: "I'm not elated or anything like that. I lost a lot of money. Everybody suffered, but it's time to get back to business."

More or less, Winfield's sentiments were a distillation of everyone else's. He just wanted to get back into pinstripes and resume the season.

"I'll pick up just where I left off," he promised. "I'm in shape. I was having the best time I've had in professional baseball."

All good things must come to an end, and in Dave Winfield's case, the end wasn't all that good.

15

The New ...
New York Yankee

The baseball strike and its resolution had produced more than a different formula for free-agent compensation. As owners and player representatives were picking up the pieces, they also devised some new elements to be injected into the game, temporarily, at least.

First, the players had to get back into shape. Almost all had kept their weight down, done some jogging, perhaps thrown a ball around, but they had to come back up to game conditions. Therefore, a ten-day period was allowed, a second spring training, as it were. The annual All-Star game would be played on August 9th, to be followed on August 10th by the resumption of the regular season.

Second, the regular season itself would be divided into two "halves," one half consisting of all those games played before the strike, the other half including post-strike games. This was important in resolving the eventual divisional championships.

The winners of each half of the season were assured of playing a short series for the divisional championship. The first-half winners were: the Yankees in the A.L. East, the Oakland Athletics in the A.L. West, the

163

Philadelphia Phillies in the N.L. East and the Los Angeles Dodgers in the N.L. West.

These teams were to play their respective second-half leaders, the winners to become divisional champions. Ah, but what if the same team won both halves of the divisional race? That called for another complicated formula, but since none of the first-half winners repeated in their divisions, the solution can mercifully be left unmentioned.

The clumsiness and unfairness of this formula was best illustrated by the unfortunate Cincinnati Reds. In 1981 they had the best won-lost record (66-42) of any team in the majors, but they didn't get into any of the playoffs. Neither did the St. Louis Cardinals. They had the best overall record in the N.L. East (59-43) but it didn't mean a thing.

On the other hand, the Kansas City Royals, who had, overall, played three games under .500, had managed to win the second half of their division and did get into the playoffs.

Without doubt the "guaranteed" appearance of the four first-half winners had something to do with their second-half failures. There was no incentive for them to win, other than to fatten individual statistics. To be fair, the players were professionals and did try to win, but somehow that little spark was missing.

There was no spark missing in Dave Winfield during the All-Star game. He didn't get a hit, but the mob in Cleveland cheered like hell for attempted catches he *didn't* make.

In the seventh inning, Montreal catcher Gary Carter teed off on a Ron Davis hard one and belted it to dead center. There was no doubt in the mind of anybody in the ball park that it was gone, but Winfield didn't quite believe that. He raced to the warning track, leaped high to the top of the wall and came down empty-handed as it landed just out of reach. Had the six-six outfielder been a mite taller, he might have had it.

Then, in the eighth inning, Mike Schmidt took a fancy to one of Rollie Fingers' offerings and clobbered it in the same direction. Again Winfield did his climbing act, banging into the wall, and again it was barely inches over his reaching glove.

That was the same Dave Winfield who had been castigated in San Diego because "he refused to go to the wall." In fact it was Rollie Fingers who had said it. He couldn't say it anymore.

"I'm not trying to get hurt out there," Winfield said quietly, "but I've got to go for it."

If Winfield was ready to go in the second half, he certainly didn't show it. Often enough he put good wood on the ball, but now it wasn't falling in as it had before. He began to press, exhibiting all the overanxious faults he'd shown during March spring training, and the slump only deepened. Over the first 16 days of the second half he batted an anemic .143 and his overall average plunged accordingly.

Gene "Stick" Michael stuck with Winfield because Dave was not the only player skidding; the whole team was playing in-and-out baseball. They'd look terrible in some games, then start a winning streak, only to fall back into the same aimless pattern. Some sportswriters accused the Yanks of coasting out the season, since they'd be in the playoffs even if they finished last in their division over the second half.

Steinbrenner didn't take kindly to such criticism and he blistered his players, a tactic he resorted to on a number of occasions. After one shoddy game against the White Sox, the boss uttered a few well-chosen words, then ordered a workout on what should have been a day off. When Michael told Steinbrenner the players could use a rest, George III took off against his manager. The workout was held as the boss had ordered, but the players weren't very happy.

"George sent Bill Bergesch [a Yankee executive] to the workout to make sure each guy bunted 15 times," one player said sourly. "Do you think Stick Michael would have made us do that? No way. He had to send his man there to make sure everybody bunted."

Few fans can understand the pressure on a manager when the owner is unhappy. Some go to extremes that are almost comical. Charley Finley, when he owned the Oakland A's, was known to call his manager in the dugout during a game with specific instructions, and woe betide the manager who failed to follow orders to the letter. If Finley ordered a squeeze play with the bases loaded, nobody out, and the meat of his batting order due up, the manager's best choice was the squeeze play, and he forgot about a potential big inning. Finley was also known to call his manager at three or four o'clock in the morning to demand a play-by-play explanation of the manager's strategy, and then he would offer his own critique.

To a certain extent Steinbrenner was cut from the same cloth. He, too, would second-guess his managers, make calls early in the morning, and in general make his presence felt. When Dick Howser managed the Yankees in 1980, the team won 103 games, the most in baseball, but because they lost out to Kansas City in the playoffs, Howser fell into disfavor. After a period of recriminations, Howser "resigned." He was replaced by Michael.

Supposedly, Gene Michael was "Steinbrenner's boy." Graceful, slender (that was how he got his nickname, "Stick"), Michael had been a "good field–no hit" shortstop, but a man with a keen insight into baseball. In 1979 he had managed the Yankees' Columbus, Ohio, Triple A farm team to a championship and was appointed general manager of the Yankees for 1981. A low-key person, Stick seldom let off steam, but when he did, he meant every word he said and devil take the hindmost. He absorbed the boss's blasts as long as he could and then spoke his mind.

"If Steinbrenner wants to fire me, then let him fire me," was all he said.

It was enough.

In September, Michael was relieved of command and in marched Bob Lemon.

It was not the first time Lemon had been called on to finish out the season at the helm. A couple of years earlier, Billy Martin got into an argument with Steinbrenner and was told to go home; Lemon finished out the season. When the rotund former pitching great made his appearance for the second time in the same role, one scribe snickered, "I've heard of relief pitchers, but not until now did I hear of a relief manager."

For Dave Winfield it must have been a case of déjà vu. He had been through the same scenes in San Diego—the team owner who let loose a blast at his team, the firing of managers in midseason or in spring training (Roger Craig, Alvin Dark). Only there was one big difference: the Padres would not improve in spite of the tantrums, the Yankees would. It was merely a ploy to shake them out of their lethargy. It was too good a team.

Winfield had waited a long time to go home to the Twin Cities as a major leaguer. He had no opportunity while he played with the Padres because the Twins are an American League team, and the first Yankee-Twins game, scheduled for June, had been canceled because of the strike. Early in September he was in the Twin Cities.

Long ago, while attending the university, Winfield had ridden the busses when he needed transportation. There had been no extra money at home for the luxury of even a beat-up secondhand set of wheels. But now he was behind the steering wheel of a sleek silver Mercedes, tooling it into the parking lot of the Minnesota State Fair, one of the largest such exhibits in the country. It was a memorable homecoming.

At the fair Dave wandered through the flower and farm buildings; then he tried his throwing arm at a booth where objects on a shelf had to be knocked down to win a prize. Grinning from ear to ear, he came up empty as he felled only two of the targets, missing the third.

"That can't be Winfield," yelled someone in the crowd.

"People notice you," he remarked. "The people who remember me from Minnesota probably recall that I played basketball, not baseball. Had I still been playing for the Padres, I wouldn't have been as recognized."

Dave had two parties in mind and he hosted both. First was the one for the kids. The Winfield Foundation invited 1,500 kids to a game, and provided all the usual trappings that went with it: the medical examination, the picnic supper, and seats in right field. With Dave, right field was a tradition even though he now played in left field. But the kids didn't mind a hoot, because they could ogle Reggie Jackson, who was doing a little time-step between innings to a John Denver tune and helping the cause with a nice diving catch.

The next party was for his teammates, out at his St. Paul home, for some vittles and music. There he reminisced about the Minnesota Twins of old, about Harmon Killebrew and Tony Oliva, two of his idols, and how he had cherished a mental picture of himself out there in the ball park in Bloomington.

"The kids of today still look at us like I looked at those guys," he said. "Only it's not exactly what you think it will be. Once you play for a number of years and look around, it's not all glory. Sure, I'm having a great time, but the pressure of New York and a Yankee uniform is unbelievable."

Winfield had been struggling at bat until the Twins series, but he came alive before his home town folks. In the first game he had a pair of singles and a run-scoring double. In the next game he had two hits.

The finale of the series was not so pleasant. With the Yanks clinging to a precarious 3-2 lead in the bottom of the eighth and one out, Hosken Powell looped a short fly to left. Shortstop Larry Milbourne raced out, Winfield charged in, and Winfield dropped it. A triple and a suicide squeeze gave the Twins the lead and the game.

"I came a long way and it hit off my glove," Dave said sadly. "If I reach a ball, if I get my glove on it, I should catch it. No excuses. It cost us a game."

Late in the season Winfield was stunned when he received the first of a series of communications from some of the crackpots who infest every city. It was a letter, with a photograph of Dave attached, and it read:

"You're going to get hurt, either in the outfield or at bat. You will not be playing in the playoffs or in the games in the World Series if New York makes the Series. Each day you will be aware of what might happen. No one wishes to be hurt but it's going to happen. So many people make so little for so much more important work. Nigger, you'll get yours."

Rick Cerone asked for and received special police and bodyguards when he received a death threat. "You try not to let it bother you," he said, but it was obvious that such idiocy had added to the tension.

Reggie Jackson was almost used to such moronic threats. "It's a very unfortunate thing," he shook his head. "I used to get them every year when I was playing in Oakland. A friend of mine, an FBI agent, practically lived at my house when this happened. Well, what's the difference? If you're going to die, you're going to die. And if you're going to die, the Man Upstairs has got the itinerary all laid out for you. You can't do anything about it."

Willie Randolph was somewhat more somber about the death-threat business. "I guess we all live in constant fear," he said. "I sometimes wonder if there's someone up there in the upper deck with a gun or a rifle. Or some of those people who run up to you at the end of a game. Most of those people are real happy. They're real fans. But you never know if one of those guys is going to run up to you and stick a knife into you."

Manager Bob Lemon, who had been in baseball for a long time, observed, "You have to handle these things as they come up. There's so much bullshit with these death threats." But, as the cowardly threats against Winfield's life continued, Lemon added, "It's bad to get these things at any time. It's *real* bad to get them when you're headed for the playoffs or the World Series."

And Winfield was continuing to receive them. Via telephone, a message came to Frohman for relaying to Dave: "You tell that mother-fucker he's dead."

In the mail: "You'll never get to the end of the World Series. Bang."

Without doubt Winfield was upset—probably frightened, as any sensible man would be—but he put up a brave front. "I'm going out to play, and we're going to kick their butts. I'm not going to be intimidated by death threats."

The split season wound down and finished, much to the relief of the owners, the players, and the fans. The whole thing had left a residue of ill will among all parties, especially the fans, who saw inflated salaries spread among the players, nice profits for the owners, and rising ticket prices in the future for those who paid the ultimate bills.

For Dave Winfield, 1981 had been a season of fulfillment. After that initial miserable start in the second half, he had batted .300 the rest of the way, finishing at .294, second in batting, among the regulars, only to former Padre Jerry Mumphrey's .306. He led the Yankees in hits, total bases, doubles, runs batted in, game-winning hits, and scoring sacrifice flies. His 13 home runs were second to Graig Nettles and Reggie Jackson, who tied at 15 each. Aside from that weak getaway, there had neen a consistency about his stickwork, evidenced by two 9-game hitting streaks and 26 multiple-hit games.

Before joining the Yankees, Winfield remarked that he had played in few important games during his career. The first time he was in a major league uniform was important, as were the All-Star games, but the rest of the games were relatively meaningless. Always, when the last out of the regular season had been recorded, he packed up and went away. Now he was about to participate in his first postseason contest, a thrill he had longed for since June of 1973.

The Yankees defeated the Milwaukee Brewers in the best-3-out-of-5 series to take the divisional title, but not before Steinbrenner got a few things off his chest. The Yanks won the first two, then lost the following pair, igniting the boss's fuse and causing him to mutter darkly about breaking up the Yankees. Perhaps Steinbrenner's veiled threats worked, or maybe the Yankees were just the better team. They won it by coming from behind. Before the wrapup Jackson had said, "I keep hearing about how great I am in the clutch. Well, if I'm ever to do anything, it ought to be tonight."

Mr. October hit a home run. The Yanks won, 7-3.

Everybody in baseball was looking forward to the confrontation between Steinbrenner and Billy Martin when the Oakland A's came to town to tussle for the American League pennant. They were probably expecting a variation of the shootout at the O.K. Corral, because nothing would have pleased Martin more than taking the title away from his former employer, and Steinbrenner would never have heard the last of it if he lost.

Much had been written about Billy Martin's success as a manager, and most of it was true. He had a hair-trigger temper; those arguments he couldn't settle with words he resolved with his fists. Certain incidents in which he displayed his wrath have been recorded on video tape for posterity, the classic among them being the scene in which he kicked dirt over an umpire's shoes, and when the ump turned his back on him, Billy picked up handfuls of dirt and tossed them at the arbiter's back.

But nobody could take away from him his ability to get the best out of his personnel. Usually he was handed a bunch of losers, and without fail he turned them into winners. Martin's baseball knowledge had been learned at the knee of Casey Stengel, perhaps the most innovative manager of all. As a major league player, Martin was merely adequate; as a manager, there was none better.

Minnesota was Martin's first club, in 1969. The team had finished seventh the previous year. Martin took them to first place in the A.L. West, but got himself fired after a dispute with owner Calvin Griffith.

Detroit followed. In two seasons he maneuvered that bunch of also-rans to second place and then first place in the A.L. East. But the ambitious Billy wanted a bigger contract, which he surely deserved, and he also got his name in the headlines too often. The front office waved bye-bye to Billy.

Next came the Texas Rangers. They had lost 105 games, which was sufficient reason to fire the previous manager, Whitey Herzog. Under Martin's guidance Texas finished second in the A.L. West, only five games behind Oakland. But the team changed ownership, Martin and general manager Dan O'Brien were reportedly feuding, and Martin was out. A job with the Yankees showed up and he grabbed it. That had been his destination in the first place.

It was then that New York fans got their first extended look at a brand of baseball that later became known as "Billy ball." It was nothing more than sound fundamentals combined with daring on the base paths. Billy had the players who could hit the ball out of the park, but he was not above using them to execute a suicide squeeze play. Chris Chambliss, then the Yankee first baseman and an occasional long-ball hitter, did exactly that in one game, throwing consternation into the ranks of the enemy.

Martin's success with the Yankees was highlighted by close encounters with Steinbrenner and Reggie Jackson. On one occasion, in full view of a television audience, Martin almost came to blows with Jackson in the Yankee dugout, and only the intervention of the late Elston Howard prevented blood on the cement floor. After Martin's celebrated one-punch fight with a marshmallow salesman in Minneapolis, Steinbrenner fired his flamboyant manager—for the second time.

That was the hardest blow Martin had to absorb in his professional career. Billy had an all-consuming love affair with the Yankees, ever since he had broken in as a brash rookie. He was thoroughly steeped in pin stripe tradition, a tradition Dave Winfield was only beginning to observe and understand.

Martin showed up finally as manager of the Oakland Athletics in 1980. Donning an A's cap for the cameras, he flatly predicted that the team would be challenging for the division title. At the time it seemed that Billy had shot off his mouth once too often. He was about to assume command of a bunch of clowns, whose destiny, almost everyone believed, was to challenge Seattle for sole possession of the cellar in the A.L. West.

But Martin made good his boast. The Athletics finished second to Kansas City in 1980. In 1981, he knocked the Royals off in the opening round of playoffs to take the A.L. West title. Then he led his troops into Yankee Stadium for a confrontation with his former peerless general, George Steinbrenner.

The Yankees won the first game, 3-1. Winfield did not particularly distinguish himself; he was just in the game. In the following contest he was *the* star among stars.

Tony Armas, Oakland's right fielder, led off the second inning with a long clout, headed for the left field bleachers. At the crack of the bat Winfield raced to the wall, uncoiled like a compressed spring, leaped high up against the wall, and snatched the ball right out of the second row.

As the home town throng roared with delight and amazement, Billy Martin said graciously, "Dave Winfield made one of the greatest plays I've seen in many years."

Winfield's catch was almost a carbon copy of the one he had made at Yankee Stadium on September 24th, when he victimized Doug De-Cinces of the Orioles with a practically identical grab. Later, he commented on both catches.

"The one DeCinces hit was on an angle and I could see it better. But Armas's drive was hit right at me, it had no angle; the ball was right in the sun and had overspin. I guess I'm the only one tall enough or crazy enough to try it."

In the bottom of the fourth, with the score knotted at 3-all, Winfield came to bat with the bases loaded, and he rocketed a one-hop double off the wall to chase home a pair of runs, which proved to be the winning markers. He also got a single in the Yankees' productive seventh inning. It was a 13-3 laugher for the Yanks.

Winfield's elation came bubbling up. Asked how he felt after performing so well in a playoff game, Dave replied, "I would have done it a long time ago but I never had the chance. No one knew about my ability before I came to New York. I talked about it in San Diego, but no one wanted to hear it. I guess it was taboo to say you were good out there."

That was Wednesday, October 14, 1981. It was to be Dave Winfield's final day of glory that season. He would not enjoy the spotlight when it shone on him again.

The Yankees went on to sweep the Athletics in Oakland and wrap up the American League pennant. But there was no champagne in the clubhouse to celebrate the victory, because, as Steinbrenner put it, "We haven't won it all yet. One more to go."

Steinbrenner did host a party for his players at an Oakland restaurant, and it was there that Winfield learned that the Yanks rooted for each other on the field, but when they weren't under game conditions, all was not love and pink roses.

Fisticuffs among the Yankees was not unknown. In one celebrated act of violence (or maybe it was merely fun-loving horseplay in the showers), a substitute catcher named Cliff Johnson broke the thumb of ace reliever Goose Gossage, putting the righthander on the disabled list for a long time, and eventually costing the Yanks the pennant.

This time Graig Nettles and Reggie Jackson went at each other. According to several reports, Jackson invited some of his friends to the party and they sat down at Nettles' table. Nettles took exception to their presence, got up from the table and went looking for Jackson. Both players stepped out of the dining room to discuss the matter. Supposedly, Nettles was holding a beer bottle. Also supposedly, Jackson slapped the bottle out of his hand. A third supposition had it that Nettles knocked Jackson down with a punch to the mouth. Any version of the incident also included the fact that there was little love between Nettles and Jackson. Nettles didn't care much for Reggie's constant display of ego.

The Yankees and Dodgers faced off in the World Series, with the Yankees winning the first two. Although he didn't know it yet, Dave Winfield was starting to sink out of sight in the worst slump of his career.

In the final playoff game against Oakland, Winfield had gone 0-for-5. In the opener against Los Angeles he was 0-for-3, and in the second game, 0-for-4.

The Dodgers, as they had done all season long and in the National League playoffs, came fighting back to win the third game, 5-4. The Yanks had rookie sensation Fernando Valenzuela on the ropes early, but couldn't quite put him away. The young Latin hung on gamely to take the decision. Winfield went 0-for-3.

Los Angeles went on to tie the Series, 8-7, in game number four. Reggie Jackson was both the hero and the goat. He got on base five times with a homer, two singles, and two walks. He also dropped a fly ball in the sixth inning that permitted the Dodgers to rally. The Yankees collected 13 hits. Winfield went 0-for-4. He did draw two walks.

Other good hitters had experienced dreadful slumps in World Series competition. Gil Hodges, once a great first baseman for the Brooklyn Dodgers, had known the misery of the horse collar. Hodges was one of the most popular of all Brooklyn players, and he had fans going to church and praying for him, but nothing seemed to work. Hodges bore it with a stoicism that showed what a truly classy guy he was. His teammates, to a man, suffered with him.

George Steinbrenner, however, was not enchanted with the deeds of his new left fielder. He told the press, "The guy we depend on isn't producing one bit . . . two hits in about two weeks."

Not until the fifth inning of game five, which the Yankees also lost, did Winfield break the ice with a single. It was to be his only hit of the Series. Then, standing on first base, he did something which might have been a self-mocking gesture, or perhaps he had a sudden silly desire for a souvenir: He asked for the ball!

It was an ill-advised request. The fans and the media got on him for that.

George Steinbrenner came away from Los Angeles with three unsought souvenirs of his visit: a swollen lip, a bruise on his head, and a cast on his left hand, all the result of an altercation with a couple of Los Angeles fans in a hotel elevator.

According to Steinbrenner's version of what happened, he was alone in the elevator at about eight o'clock when the two men got on. One had a beer bottle, the other held the door. The man holding the beer bottle recognized Steinbrenner and cast aspersions on him and his team. Harsh words were exchanged, whereupon the man hit George on the head with the bottle. Steinbrenner retaliated by decking the guy with a punch. The other chap let one fly at Steinbrenner and he too got a few knuckles in his face.

A couple of minor tremors had shaken the Los Angeles area during the Yankees' stay. Boarding the plane for the return flight, Steinbrenner looked at his hand and remarked, "What more could have happened to us in L.A.? Two earthquakes, three losses, and now this."

Game six was the finale and the Yankees were shot down in flames. There would be second-guessing of managerial strategy, bad base running, a question regarding the benching of Jerry Mumphrey during part of the Series, but none of it mattered. The Yankees, after winning the first two games, had been taken out in four straight. It was a humiliating experience.

At the beginning of the season, Winfield had been interviewed by a sportswriter for *Sport Magazine,* and one series of questions proved more prophetic than anyone suspected at the time.

"Suppose you have a great season and then go 0-for-12 in the playoffs. Can you accept the screaming that will come?" the queries started.

"How do you know there will be screaming?" Winfield countered.

"Why do you think Steinbrenner will treat you differently from Reggie or any of the other guys?"

To which Winfield replied, "Steinbrenner went after me and is paying me so much that if he screams at me it's like screaming at himself. Besides, I'm not frightened. There's plenty of cotton in the drugstores."

The 1981 World Series had been a disaster for Dave Winfield. He went 1-for-22, a batting average of .045. He drove in only one run, not with his bat but via a bases-loaded walk. Winfield decided he could do nothing but apologize to the boss.

"He told me, 'I know I let you down. I embarrassed you, but it won't happen again,'" Steinbrenner told reporters. "He brought us here, but he had a bad Series, that's all. The Series is a different experience for everybody, especially the first time. Willie Wilson realized that last year when he struck out 13 times for the Royals."

Win or lose, George Steinbrenner had made his point long ago, that he always hired the best players for the Yankees—his "Mona Lisa," as he called the team—and almost always they delivered. Catfish Hunter got off to a poor start in his first season with the Yanks, but ended up at 23-14. Reggie Jackson, in his debut year, hit .286 with 32 home runs and 110 runs batted in. Goose Gossage, in his maiden Yankee effort, had a 2.01 earned run average with 27 saves.

Winfield had merely reversed the procedure. He had started off with a bang and ended with a whimper. But, like his first season with the Padres, his initial year as a Yankee was a learning experience.

"Failure," said George Steinbrenner, discussing the World Series with a sportswriter, "is only worthwhile if it's a learning experience. I think it was for Dave Winfield. I look for him to be one of our great ones, and I want to repeat," said George, "I also realize that Dave was the guy who brought us to the Series."

"I tried like hell to do the things I did all year," said Dave. "If I knew what happened, believe me, I'd have tried to rectify them. What I needed was a couple of papier-mâché hits like the Dodgers got. It just didn't happen for me."

"I feel all right," he said, "My head's up. It should be. If I'd have played any harder this year I might be dead. You know," he added, "I wouldn't have cared a damn about getting no hits, if we'd won the Series. I have a lot of respect for this city, for this team, and for the name of the team. I really know how to be proud of wearing Yankee pin-stripes now. You talk about being proud? Damn right I'm proud. It took one year to become part of a great tradition."

A complex man, Dave Winfield. He is a proud man with a wide streak of humility. He is a winner who also has learned to take defeat philosophically, without allowing defeat to destroy him. He is an individualist who can subordinate his individualism for the good of the team and he is a generous man with an understanding of the needs of others.

Dave Winfield is a baseball hero. More importantly, Dave Winfield is his own man, a man of honesty and integrity, and certainly, as he wishes most, a model for youngsters, anywhere and in whatever walk of life, to emulate.

Since Reggie Jackson has gone—to the Angels—a number of shrewd baseball observers think that George Steinbrenner has recast the Yankees in a kind of "Dave Winfield image." An image with speed, dash, hustle, and fiery play, and only occasional power to hit the long ball. A new kind of "Yankee-ball." That remains to be seen.

For Dave Winfield . . . his career is just beginning.

His greatest years still lie ahead. . . .

Index